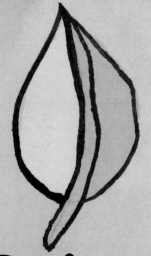

Colorful Stitchery

65 Hot Embroidery Projects to Personalize Your Home

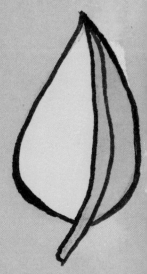

KRISTIN NICHOLAS

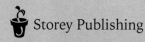

Storey Publishing

The mission of Storey Publishing is to serve our customers by publishing practical information that encourages personal independence in harmony with the environment.

For my dad,
Archibald Nicholas, Jr.,
who lived a colorful life
full of passions.
Dad, you taught us all
that passion is vital
to a life well lived.

Edited by Gwen Steege
Art direction and cover design by Kent Lew
Text design by Cynthia McFarland
Text production by Jennie Jepson Smith
Cover photographs by Kevin Kennefick, except for author photograph, reprinted with permission, Meredith Corporation ©, Country Home Magazine®, September 2005. Photographer, John Gruen.
Interior photographs by Kevin Kennefick, with the exception of the details of the stitchery on pages 53–55, 59–61, 63–65, 71–73, 75–76, 79–81, 84–85, 88–89, 91–95, 97–99, 102, 104–5, 110, 112, 117, 120–21, 124–25, 131–33, 136–40, 143, 147, 150–51, 154, 159, 163–65, 168–69, 171, 173, 176–77 by Adam Mastoon
Photo styling by Wendy Scofield
Patterns and Diagrams by Lindsay Janeczek
Indexed by Chris Lindemer, Boston Road Communications
Copyright © 2005 by Kristin Nicholas
Illustrations © 2005 by Kristin Nicholas

The information in this book is true and complete to the best of our knowledge. All recommendations are made without guarantee on the part of the author or Storey Publishing. The author and publisher disclaim any liability in connection with the use of this information. For additional information please contact Storey Publishing, 210 MASS MoCA Way, North Adams, MA 01247.

Storey books are available for special premium and promotional uses and for customized editions. For further information, please call 1-800-793-9396.

Printed in the United States by Von Hoffmann

10 9 8 7 6 5 4 3 2 1

LIBRARY OF CONGRESS CATALOGING-IN-PUBLICATION DATA

Nicholas, Kristin.
  Colorful stitchery / by Kristin Nicholas.
    p. cm.
  Includes index.
  ISBN-13: 978-1-58017-611-8; ISBN-10: 1-58017-611-9 (pbk. : alk. paper)
  1. Embroidery — Patterns. I. Title.

TT771.N488 2005
746.44′041—dc22

2005022261

Contents

I come from a family of women — lots of them. Growing up, I loved it — the female energy, the sharing and caring, and all the projects we made together, mostly done with a needle and thread. There was a long line of needlewomen in both my mother's and father's families. My grandmother Frieda came from Germany with her parents in 1910. My grandmother and great-grandmother spent their lives creating things with their hands. They stitched clothes, embroidered pillowcases, crocheted afghans, tatted red, white and blue hankies during World War II, and filled every sofa with beautiful afghans. They weren't alone. All their friends stitched, gathering together in a sewing circle every week for more than 50 years to mend, knit, crochet, embroider, or quilt.

My Life in Stitches

I grew up in a medium-size town in northern New Jersey in a family of five girls. Around us, farms were still growing fruits and vegetables and animals. A beehive of activity and creativity, the home my mom and dad presided over was unlike many in the town. My four sisters and I were always stitching or baking something. We frequently taught our friends how to make the craft of the moment. I sewed all my clothes and proudly wore them to school. I despised going clothes shopping (and still do) and knew I could make an outfit that was better and cost less than what I could buy, and I could look different from everyone else at school.

When I flew the comfortable coop and went to college, I chose to study textiles and clothing design. As far as I was concerned, there was nothing else I should study. Textiles, and all the stitching, creating, color, and texture, had filled my life. I was serious about textiles and wanted to learn more.

I arrived at university in the mid-70s. My dorm was a big, old brick building oozing with East Coast charm, complete with sweeping porches and overstuffed chairs in the common room. Little did I know, but my dorm was a "women's studies" dorm. Women's liberation was in full swing, and I didn't know a thing

about it. Women were experimenting with ideas they'd never dreamed of, men were running scared *or* rejoicing, and bras were going up in smoke. It's hard to explain now what women were going through at that time in history. We were becoming empowered and were planning to take over the world. Females were banding together to take our place next to men in the working world, to become equals. And it was a real struggle.

When I arrived, all I wanted to do was to study textiles and clothing design, sew beautiful fabrics, and learn as much as I could about everything to do with textiles, but I quickly caught on to the currents of the moment. I became embarassed about my course of study and kept my sewing skills in the closet. There was a stigma attached to the School of Home Economics: The common impression was that all those students were learning to cook and clean, make clothing, raise a family, and find a husband. The nicknames for Home Ec students were "Becky Home-Ecky" and "Suzy Home-maker." These were not compliments.

I knew differently. I knew that I could study textiles and turn my skills into a legitimate career, still stay with the times and become a "professional" woman. I had to follow my instincts and keep on stitching, keeping my passions quiet, and plow on to learn all I could. I re-taught myself to knit from a paperback book on a cross-country train trip. I continued sewing

and embroidering, learned to weave and print fabric and identify fibers under a microscope. I learned to make my own sewing patterns and to drape fabric on a mannequin into beautiful dresses. And I learned about all kinds of art — photography, drawing, color, and, especially, the then newly coined term "fiberart." I discovered that if I called those stitching crafts I was so enamored of *fiberart*, I was then legitimate: an artist and no longer Becky Home-Ecky. I met Vera Kaminski, the Fiber Professor and a feminist. Vera introduced me to Judy Chicago and her Dinner Party. Vera built a womb out of fiber and installed it at art galleries. I, too, could be a feminist and it was okay to do what I loved — know how to stitch!

And so now, here I am, almost 30 years later. During those 30 years I've continued to stitch and sew and knit. I built a valid career around textiles as creative director of a yarn company for almost 20 years. I've studied more textiles than I ever could have imagined. I visit museums and view historic textiles. I scour flea markets for beautiful old fabrics. I rush to any folk art or ethnic exhibit I can find. I wonder about the lives of the people who made those incredible textiles. I know they didn't have hot water or indoor toilets, to say nothing of factory-spun yarn or stores to purchase fabric at. The history of a single piece of stitched textiles continues to fuel my imagination. I don't think it will ever stop.

I'm a romantic at heart. I love beauty, softness, music, interpersonal relationships, colors, art, nature, comfy sofas and pillows, a roaring fire, and yarn and fabric. For me, everything about textiles is romantic. I think about the sheep that grew the wool for my yarn, the shepherd that kept watch over the flock and helped birth all those lambs, the shearer that removed the coat so the sheep could grow some more. I think about natural dyes grown and gathered by people way-back-when to color their wool. I think about the mothers who taught their daughters to stitch, to weave the fabric, and to make the clothes they wore on their farms. I think of the cycle of life that continues today in villages across the world. I realize the important bartering power that stitching embroidered fabrics earns the women in faraway villages to purchase things they can't make. I think about the designs and stitches that have traveled the world from village to village, from woman to woman. It still captivates and fascinates me.

So now, in our current mass-media culture full of computers, downloaded files, and visual over-stimulation, our popular culture has come full circle. "They" (the mass media) have discovered knitting and crafting! It's suddenly hip to knit and stitch! Well, thank goodness it is. Knitting and stitching could save the world. Think about all the world leaders sitting together with needles and wool yarn slowly looping or weaving it in and out. They would all calm down, find some inner peace, enjoy the rhythm of the needle, the building of the pattern. They would slowly discuss the problems of the world and establish reasonable solutions. They would talk about their villages, their families. They would realize we're all alike trying to find our place in the world, trying to create a little romance and beauty with a needle and thread. They would find out what I learned as a child: that a little stitching helps to solve the world's problems — or maybe just the problems of my day.

Stitching is a life in its own. It will hold you together when you're falling apart. It will enable you to solve your problems as you skillfully move a needle through fabric or loop yarn into stitches. I can't live without stitching. It has become the one constant in my life that I always carry around with me, to all reaches of the globe. I remember where I was when I was making a particular project. I remember the people I've met and the sights I've seen. Stitching can do the same for you — it can make you feel useful in new ways. You'll be able to share your stitches with others, in the form of beautiful handmade gifts you put your love into or even in the form of teaching the craft to others. So explore what there is to offer and begin a stitched life you'll learn to love.

Kristin Nicholas

All's Well That Begins Well

You are about to embark on a journey — a good journey others have traveled before you. People have been stitching for thousands of years, even when it wasn't so easy to gather the supplies they needed. Prehistoric stitchers sewed on animal skins with bone needles and sinew. Until not so long ago, fiber had to be grown, spun, and woven into fabric before decorative stitchery could even begin. Needles were forged from silver or other metals. It's a wonder anyone ever stitched decoratively at all! Yet museums all over the world include samples of decorative embroidery on ancient clothing, pictures, and household textiles. Today, on the other hand, it's very easy and inexpensive to get into stitchery. A visit to your local craft or needlework store and a few dollars sets you up. Another visit to a fabric store and you're stocked with fabrics to stitch on. A few simple supplies will keep you busy for years!

In these pages, you'll learn how to choose ground fabrics (what your stitches are made on), as well as about threads to stitch with and useful tools that help you succeed. Lastly, you'll have 65 fun and fanciful projects to try with your needle and thread. So, turn on your favorite music, brew up a pot of tea, and read on to start your stitchery adventure. I encourage you to bring your own sense of curiosity, creativity, and style to everything you stitch!

Choosing your ground fabric can be the most fun, though sometimes the most challenging, part of the project. Once you get interested in stitchery, you'll find yourself looking at all kinds of fabrics from an entirely different perspective. Would this color work in my home? What could I do with this plaid — or these stripes? Would I enjoy working with this texture? Your fabric choice determines the style of the finished project — crisp and clean, warm and cozy, or sophisticated and elegant.

falling for fabrics

Be sure to keep in mind that whatever fabric you choose must be easy to poke a threaded needle through. If it isn't easy, every stitch you take will be sheer agony. Equally important, ensure that the fabric feels good in your hands. Because you're going to be holding this fabric the whole time you stitch on it, you'd better love the tactile sensation you get from it. And finally, you have to love its color.

First, examine the weave of the fabric. Are the individual threads that go over and under each other so jam-packed that a needle may never get through? Hold the fabric up to the light: Does the light pour through it, or is there only a little bit of space between the threads? If there's a lot of light, chances are you can stitch through it. On the other hand, the weave in a 250-thread-count percale sheet (thread count refers to the threads per inch in the weave) is spaced so tightly that you'd fight each stitch, and the stitching wouldn't be fun. Now, thread a needle and try poking it through the fabric to see how hard it is to pull through. If the needle slides smoothly and easily through, the material passes the needle-and-thread test.

I prefer stitching on natural-fiber fabrics like linen, cotton, wool, and silk. Natural-fiber fabrics feel good, they sew and iron beautifully, and they are forgiving. On the contrary, polyester and acrylic fabrics are often almost impossible to manipulate, and puckers stay in them forever. Although even natural-fiber fabrics may look messy and lumpy when I'm finished stitching, the steam or water I use to block the project (see page 21) helps even out irregularities and the finished piece looks perfect. Best of all, natural-fiber fabrics, especially wools and silks, absorb dye beautifully, giving me a plethora of the vibrant colors I love to stitch on.

LINEN, A TRADITIONAL STITCHERY FAVORITE

My favorite fabric to embroider on is 100 percent linen, the traditional choice of many longtime stitchers. Many of the pillows in the book are made of suit-weight linens from a fabric store. Choose a linen that is thick enough so any *floats* (threads that you carry across the back side of the fabric) won't show through. Some linens, such as handkerchief linens, are just too thin. Linen is easy to stitch on, because when you insert the needle, the threads separate and it slides right through.

COTTONS AND VEGETABLE-FIBER BLENDS

If you can't find linen fabric, look for pure cotton, a linen–cotton blend, or a hemp blend, making sure it isn't too tightly woven. Fabrics designed for quilting are a good choice, and they're available in oodles of colors. Interior-decorating fabrics are also great for embroidery. They're heavier than clothing-weight fabrics, so they have enough body and heft to make the fabric easy to stitch on. Make sure, however, that the back side isn't coated with a plastic- or rubberlike finish.

WOOL, A STITCHER'S NATURAL

I love to embroider wool fabrics, including felted wool. Wool comes in beautiful colors, it's thicker than most cottons, it has great texture, and it's so easy to stitch on. Fabric made from wool is resilient, meaning that when the fabric stretches, it bounces back to its original size, a feature sometimes called memory. This makes it a great choice for beginners. Best of all, wool is a renewable resource, because the fleece comes from sheep, which are also beautiful animals!

size matters

Wash all washable fabrics before you begin stitching on them. Washing makes the fabric softer and removes the sizing (a finish applied during manufacturing). Another plus: If there's any shrinkage, it happens before you measure, embroider, and assemble your project, so there will be no unpleasant surprises later.

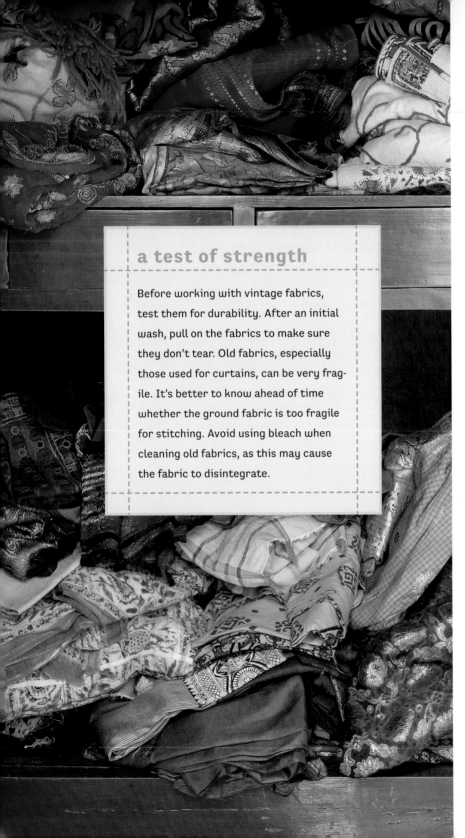

DON'T BOX YOURSELF IN

You can stitch on any fabric, including burlap and silk, in almost any pattern, including plaids, checks, and prints. You can stitch on paper and cardboard. You can stitch on leather and metal. I've even seen stitchery on porcelain. The only criterion is that you can make a hole in the material and pull the thread through it. Be creative, break rules — that's what they're for!

THE HUNT IS HALF THE FUN

Learn to look for fabric in non-conventional places. The secret to sourcing fabulous ground fabrics is to keep your eyes and mind open. You can find the most beautiful fabrics in the world in thrift shops, yard sales, and even your own — or your parents', spouse's, or friends' — closet. The Internet is another resource: Type the keywords "vintage fabric" or "antique linen" into an auction search engine, such as eBay, and you may find yourself bidding on all kinds of interesting fabrics for your stitchery. Don't spend too much time surfing, however — you're learning to stitch to *escape* technology!

Perhaps you discover a 1950s-era wool coat with great color and texture at a thrift store. Buy it, cut it apart, and turn it into pillows, potholders, tea cozies, or whatever you dream up. Dig to the back of your closet. When did you last wear that sweater? It could be great for stitchery. Old pure-wool blankets are great finds. You can get many hand-embroidered projects out of one wool blanket, even if it has a few moth holes.

Garments such as full skirts, men's shirts, women's blouses, old coats, and angora, cashmere, and wool sweaters can all be cut up for stitching projects. Solid-colored, as well as patterned fabrics, such as plaids, stripes, checks, and tweeds, form an interesting backdrop for embellishment, without overwhelming the stitchery.

Flea markets and yard sales are fabulous places to find fine table linens for very low prices. Simply cut around any permanent stains, and use the fabric for pillows, napkins, or other special projects. The perfect base for embroidery, many jacquard-woven linen or cotton tablecloths feature flowered, plaid, geometric, and other interesting patterns. Enhance these subtle designs by outlining or filling them with stitchery in white-on-white or contrasting color.

If the fabric color isn't right, you can easily transform it with a little bit of ingenuity. Simply hand-dye it on top of the stove, in the sink, or in the washing machine. (See To Dye For!, page 14.)

BURN, BABY, BURN

Before you dye anything, you need to know the fiber content of the fabric — different fibers need different dyes. When you are using salvaged fabrics or remnants, chances are the fiber won't be identified. To identify mystery fabrics, do a burn test. By observing the appearance and odor of the burning fiber, you should be able to identify it. Use the chart below to experiment with fibers whose origins you know, then move on to the mystery fabrics. Here's how:

1. Cut a 2" square from the piece of fabric. Loosen a thread and unravel it. If the fabric is a knit, pull one of the individual threads and "unknit" it. Gather about ten 2" fabric threads in this way.

2. Put a lit candle in a sink, and use tweezers to hold three threads in the flame for a couple of seconds. Watch how they burn. Blow out the flame and notice what kind of residue remains. Pay attention to the smell of the burning fiber, and compare your observations to the information in the chart below.

WHAT'S THAT FIBER? — BURN TESTS

FIBER	TYPE	SOURCE	ODOR WHEN BURNED	OTHER CHARACTERISTICS
Cotton	Cellulose	Cotton plant	Like paper.	Burns fast; leaves an ash similar to paper.
Linen	Cellulose	Flax plant	Like paper.	Thread is stiffer than cotton.
Wool, mohair, cashmere, angora	Protein	Animal products	Like human hair.	Residue is a small, crunchy ball that breaks apart.
Silk	Protein	Product of silkworms	Similar to that of wool.	Individual fibers are usually quite shiny with no kink. Sometimes has a peculiar smell when you wash it.
Polyester, nylon, acrylics	Chemical	Synthetics	Like plastic.	Residue forms a hard bead (think plastic) that can't be crushed.

To Dye For!

Dyeing is a way to be creative with fabrics and yarns, so that you can produce something totally your own. You can purchase many kinds of chemical fabric dyes that will permanently color any fabric. Buy dyes from a reputable company that provides good instructions along with the dyes. (See page 178 for my favorite dye sources.)

For dyeing wools or silks, use acid dyes. Acid dyes are easy to work with, and they develop beautiful colors. They are especially made for protein fibers (including wool and silk). You need to immerse the fabric in the dye, simmer it on top of your stove with white vinegar to set the color and make the dye solution acidic: hence the name "acid dyes."

For cottons, rayons, and other vegetable fibers, use fiber-reactive Procion dyes. The Procion dye process uses cold water and salt to set the color. Because these dyes work in cold water, you can do this kind of dyeing in your washing machine.

DYEING SUCCESS TIPS

Follow the instructions supplied with the dye you've chosen, as every dye manufacturer has different directions for each particular dye. Here are some tips for successful dyeing:

✳ Completely wet the fabric in the sink before submerging in the dye bath.

✳ Don't use lumpy dye mixtures: They result in splotchy colors.

✳ Stir the cloth constantly to produce an even-colored fabric. (On the other hand, for a tie-dyed look, don't stir at all!)

✳ Use a large dyepot so fabric can "swim" freely.

✳ Remove the fabric or yarn from the dyepot when you're happy with the color, but be aware that the color will be lighter when the fabric dries. While you still have rubber gloves on, rinse any excess dye out of the fabric until the rinse water runs clear. Dry the fabric, then wash it in your washing machine to remove any additional dye that remains.

✳ If you aren't happy with the color you made, overdye it with another color until you get something you like. Begin with lighter colors and work toward darker ones: Very dark shades are impossible to alter or remove.

DYEING SAFETY TIPS

✳ **Place.** Chemical dyes are not people friendly. Dye only when small children are not present. Set aside an entire afternoon for dyeing. It is a bit messy but lots of fun.

✳ **Equipment.** Purchase a large kettle and large stirring device at a yard sale or secondhand shop and dedicate them solely to dyeing. Gather disposable mixing containers (plastic yogurt containers work great) and a plastic spoon. To ensure that no one in your house can cook up poisonous purple spaghetti, mark your equipment clearly: FOR DYES ONLY!

✳ **Protection.** Wear rubber gloves and a mask when working with chemical dyes. Follow the directions the dye company provides with the dye. Avoid breathing the powders and, after you've mixed the dye, turn on the exhaust fan.

✳ **Mixing tips.** Mix the powdered dye with a little bit of water to form a paste, then add more water until it becomes creamy. Lastly, add it to the dyepot full of water and stir. If you are dyeing an intense color, add water to the entire jar of dye, mix, and pour the whole mixture into the dyepot. (Acid dyes for wool and protein fibers come in ½-ounce jars; Procion dyes for vegetable fibers come in 2-ounce jars.)

As with fabric, you have many options when it comes to choosing stitchery threads, including not only traditional wool and cotton threads and yarns, but also silk, linen, rayon, and even more suprising materials, such as metal, ribbon, raffia, and kitchen twine you'll find in solids and multi-colors. The most important factor in choosing a thread is that you can easily pull it through your fabric. If it's lumpy and bumpy, it will not be fun to use. In addition, it shouldn't break easily, as the thread does most of the work.

picking up the threads

Classic wool. Available in hundreds of colors at needlepoint shops and many yarn stores, wool has been a traditional embroidery thread for hundreds of years. I've used Paternayan Persian, my favorite, for most projects in this book. Smooth and durable, it is sold in 8-yard skeins, in more than 400 colors. Each strand is made up of three individual plies (ends, or lengths, of yarn). You can stitch with one, two, three, or more plies to create different effects. Wool is the best choice for beginners because it hides mistakes and fills large areas quickly.

Popular cotton. Craft, fabric, and large chain stores carry two kinds of cotton threads: pearl cotton and embroidery floss.

Pearl cotton is very shiny and comes in small balls (10-gram) or twisted skeins (5-gram) at many craft and chain stores; each 5-gram skein is 27 yards long. It is available in three weights (thicknesses) — 3, 5, and 8 — with 3 being the heaviest and 5 the weight most commonly used

for stitchery. Use pearl cotton just as it comes from the ball or skein, not split. Because it's thicker than floss, use it on loosely woven fabric. It doesn't flatten easily, so you may need a needle threader to draw it through your needle.

Cotton embroidery floss is shiny and smooth, very reasonably priced, and available in hundreds of colors. It comes in 8.7-yard skeins made up of six strands of finer cotton threads. Separate one strand to use for very delicate stitchery; use all six for thicker stitches. My instructions specify how many strands to use.

Knitting yarns. Smooth wool or cotton knitting and crochet yarn is great for any kind of stitchery. Your local yarn store is a great source for it. Available in many fashionable colors, knitting yarn is quite economical to stitch with, because each skein contains many yards. Knitters and crocheters, look with new eyes at your "stash" — those leftovers or odds and ends that you've acquired but never found a use for.

You may already have many of the supplies you need for embroidery, but once you get into your new hobby, you may discover others that you can't live without. The first, of course, is your needle.

tooling around

Needles. Craft stores carry a wide variety of inexpensive needles. Purchase an assortment of types and sizes, and keep them in a dry place. Be sure the needle's eye (hole) can accommodate your thread. My favorite, and the one used in most of these projects, is a chenille needle. It has a sharp point and large eye, which easily takes most wools and cottons.

Embroidery or crewel needles, with smaller eyes and sharp points, are good with cotton floss. Use a yarn darner, which has large eyes and sharp points, for alternative fibers, like raffia or ribbon. For fabric with a very open weave, use a tapestry needle, which has a large eye and blunt point. Some needles rust, so don't store one in your project fabric.

Fabric scissors. Keep one pair dedicated to fabric, and store them in a safe place, so they don't get used for anything that might dull their blades. Take them to a knife sharpener as needed.

Craft scissors. Use these for cutting paper and other general purposes.

Embroidery scissors. These scissors are usually small, with sharp points for removing mistakes. The classic Victorian-style handles are bird-shaped, but you may also find others, such as buildings, lions' tails, or rabbits.

Fabric glue. This glue holds even when wet.

Sewing pins and a pincushion to hold them. Buy stainless pins so they won't rust. I made the pincushion shown on page 8 by cutting a 7" circle from suit-weight linen decorating it with a few easy stitches, and then gathering the fabric around a small mound of filling. I glued the stuffed ball to the inside of a pretty teacup and glued the cup to the saucer.

Thimble. A thimble can save your fingers when pushing a needle through difficult fabric.

Needle threader. A handy gadget for thick yarns.

Embroidery hoop. Available in plastic or wood, an embroidery hoop keeps the fabric taut while you stitch. (See page 45.)

Tape measure. Retractable tape measures travel nicely in your stitchery bag.

See-through gridded ruler. Available at art-supply or quilting stores, a see-through ruler comes marked with blue, red, or yellow lettering. I have a 2" × 18" ruler in each color, with each inch broken down into eight parts. It's great for quickly marking stripes of any width. By turning it 90° and matching up the lines, you can make perfect squares or rectangles.

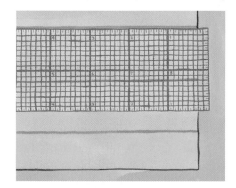

Drawing parallel lines on fabric. For a plaid, turn the ruler 90°, matching grid marks.

Masking tape. Avoid frayed edges by folding a piece of masking tape over them.

Steam iron. An essential tool when blocking.

Sewing machine. Use a sewing machine to zigzag edges to prevent fraying, as well as to assemble pillows and other items. (Fray Check prevents fraying if you don't have a machine.)

True-color light. When you work at night, it's pleasant to have a good, true-color lamp. Some come with a magnifier attached for when your eyes get tired (or old!).

COPY CATS

To transfer your design to your fabric you'll need all of the following. Most are available at craft, sewing, and quilting stores.

Dressmaker's tracing paper. Each package includes many colors, to contrast with any color fabric.

Water-soluble markers. These come only in light blue, which you can see (amazingly) on most fabric colors. After you finish stitching, simply remove marks with a squirt of water.

Child's washable markers. Not until I had a daughter did I appreciate child's washable markers! Because they come in many colors, you can use them on all colors of fabric; they're especially useful on wool or other highly textured fabrics. Be sure to get the ones labeled "washable." Although all traces are usually removable, some are tricky and require a few washings to eliminate completely. Test washability before using. Company websites supply tips for stain removal.

Black drawing pencil. Transfer designs to fabric with pencil, then remove marks with an eraser when you finish stitching.

White chalk pencil. On dark fabrics, white chalk is about the only thing that shows. Unfortunately, chalk sometimes brushes off, so you may not be able to count on it.

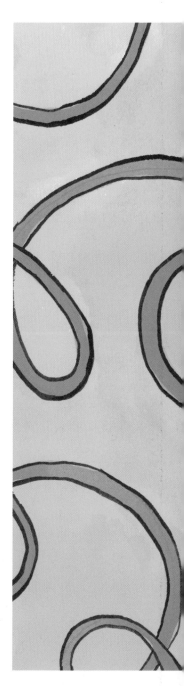

When you mention stitchery, the first thing many people think of is cross-stitch kits. Purchased kits, unfortunately, limit the stitcher to whatever designs are for sale, and many of those haven't kept up with current design trends. With this book, however, you get to choose our own ground fabric and thread. You are your own designer! You may not think so now, but you can do it, once you learn the basics and open your eyes to everything that's around you. I'll give you advice on how to transfer my designs to your fabrics, and after a little practice, you may even want to create your own designs. Think of stitchery as a fun, lifelong adventure that keeps you learning and growing creatively.

paper pattern to fabric

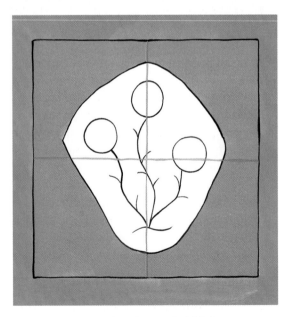

Cut-out motif being placed on marked fabric

GETTING CENTERED

Some designs should be centered on the fabric; follow these steps before beginning the transfer:

1. Cut out the square or rectangular shape for the ground fabric (see page 10).

2. To find the center of the fabric, fold it in half, matching the edges carefully, and mark the midpoint with a pin or a water-soluble or child's washable marker. Use your see-through ruler and marker to draw a straight line through the mark from edge to edge along the fold line. Fold the fabric in half in the opposite direction, mark the midpoint on the line you just drew, and draw another straight line through it from edge to edge, perpendicular to the first line. Where the two lines intersect is the center of the fabric.

3. Fold the photocopy of the design in half in both directions, matching the widest and longest parts of the design to each other. Use a light-colored marker to draw along the perpendicular lines formed by the folds.

4. Place the paper pattern on the ground fabric, matching up the vertical and horizontal lines on the paper with the vertical and horizontal lines on the fabric. Transfer by whatever method is best for your fabric. (See below.)

TRANSFERRING THE DESIGN

Before transferring your design onto your ground fabric you need to photocopy it, increasing it by the percentage required to make it actual size. (Templates for designs in this book begin on page 181; a note with each tells you what percentage increase is needed.) I use several methods to transfer the photocopy to fabric, depending on the ground fabric I've chosen.

Light table. The easiest way to transfer a design is to use a light table. Use the light-table method for most light- to medium-colored linen, cotton, and silk fabrics. Although not everyone has a light table, a window with adequate light coming through also works, or you can place a small lamp under a glass-topped table. People at a friendly camera store may let you use theirs for a minute — and that's all it takes to transfer the design to your fabric.

Tape the design to the light table or to a window on a sunny day. Place the fabric over it so the design is centered on the fabric, and tape it in place. (See Getting Centered, page 18.) Trace the design with a pencil or a water-soluble or child's washable marker.

Dressmaker's tracing paper. Use this method for wools and velvets, as well as heavy and/or dark-colored linens and cottons. Lay your fabric on a flat surface, with the colored side of the tracing paper facing the fabric. Place the photocopy of your design centered on top. Using a ballpoint pen or a pencil, draw over the design and the marks will transfer to the fabric. These marks rub off, so I usually go over the lines with a water-soluble or child's washable marker to make the design more permanent while I'm stitching. The marks rinse out once I'm done.

Photocopy transfer. Your copy shop may not know this, but I discovered that you can use a photocopy as a transfer. This method works on smooth cottons and linens. (I don't use the fabric-transfer computer paper because it leaves a plastic-like finish and the marks don't wash out. It also makes the fabric pretty unpleasant to stitch on.)

Pin the photocopy face down on your fabric and iron over it, using a cotton setting without steam. Keep the iron moving, and check after about a minute to see if the design has transferred. If the design doesn't come out dark enough, go over it with a water-soluble or child's washable marker. The ironed-on lines from the photocopy disappear under your stitching. I suggest testing this method on a scrap of fabric before using it on the project piece.

Note: You get a mirror image of your design with this method, so if you're stitching letters or anything that must be oriented in a specific direction, ask the copy shop to flip the design before you copy it.

Dividing strands out of a skein

Beginning with an overhand knot

Beginning with a rolled knot

The perfect length of thread to work with is about 30". Longer threads knot up on themselves frequently, becoming completely frustrating. They also become thinner and slightly worn toward the end if they're too long.

Persian wool yarns are skeined with three strands together, and cotton embroidery floss, with six strands. Pattern directions specify how many strands to use. To separate one or two strands from a skein, first cut the length you need. Holding the length lightly in one hand, pick up the required number of threads between the thumb and finger of your other hand and gently pull them straight out of the bundle.

Arrange the thread so that two-thirds of its length is on one side of the needle and one-third is on the other side. Make a double overhand knot ½" from the longer end, so the knot won't pull through the fabric. Or, wrap the yarn end around your finger several times, then roll the threads together as you slip them off your finger and pull to form a rolled knot (see at left).

After completing a section of stitching, or when your thread becomes too short to stitch with, pull the threaded needle to the back side. Take three tiny stitches on top of each other in the fabric to make a stitched knot, but don't let them show through on the front. (You can also use a stitched knot to begin.) Alternatively, secure thread by weaving the threaded needle through the stitches on the back (see at right).

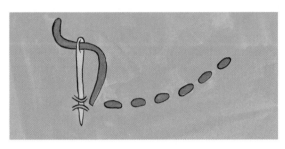

Ending with stitched knot

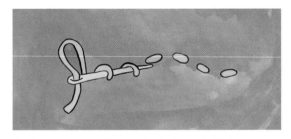

Ending by weaving through back sides of stitches

FINAL STEPS

After finishing a piece of stitchery, I rinse and sometimes block it. (For pillows, or other projects that require assembly, I do this before sewing the pieces together.) The rinsing and blocking evens out any messy stitching, removes marking lines, and gives the whole piece a more professional appearance. Although blocking improves the look of most pieces, miracles won't happen if the piece is very messy!

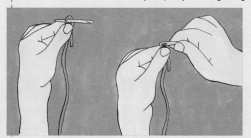
Rinsing. Immerse the fabric in cold water (no detergent) and gently swish it around for a minute or two. Remove it, and roll it in a thick, dry terry cloth towel to absorb the excess water. Lay the piece flat, stitchery-side up, to dry. You may sometimes see color in the water if dye from the threads or yarn was not properly fixed to the fiber at the factory. If this happens, quickly remove the piece and proceed as above, using a second dry towel if necessary to speed the drying process. If you're lucky, the color will not bleed into the fabric or the adjacent stitches. Manufacturers try to make all their thread colorfast, but not everyone or every dyelot is perfect. If any of your marking lines remain after rinsing, refer to the stain-removal section of the marker company's website and follow their directions.

Blocking. If the stitching is puckered, I block the piece to even it out after rinsing it. While the piece is still damp, I use large rustproof pins or tacks to pin the fabric to a corkboard or mattress covered with a thick terry cloth towel. I then pull on the fabric and the stitches to flatten out the puckers, and allow the piece to dry in this position.

Ironing. Before assembling the project, it's a good idea to iron the embroidered piece to remove all the creases in the fabric. Lay a folded terry cloth towel on an ironing board. With the right side of the stitched piece facing down against the towel, spritz it heavily with water. Using your iron set on "steam," gently press the fabric to get rid of all the wrinkles. Try not to flatten the stitchery itself too much: Part of embroidery's appeal is the texture that sits above the ground fabric.

Finished project pinned out for blocking

mastering the stitches

Remember ever using shoelaces to sew through holes punched into thick cardboard sewing cards to outline a design? This grade school project is, in fact, simple embroidery — known as *Running Stitch*. It and 20 more easy embroidery stitches are illustrated on the next few pages and featured in projects throughout the book. Each stitch is a little different, but none is difficult. Some are just plain fun and playful, and all of them are beautiful! Let your needle and thread dance across your fabric as you follow my illustrations and guidance. I've included the basics. If you really get into stitching, you may want to buy a stitch "dictionary" and explore hundreds of other possibilities.

Take an evening or two to try out all the stitches using cotton embroidery floss on a tea towel or a scrap of fabric. You'll be amazed at how easy it is to make something wonderful that looks difficult. Be patient: with each stitch your stitching will improve.

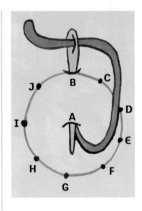

Come up in the center of the circle (A), and make a stitch from B to A. Continue in the same way to make stitches all the way around the outside of the circle to the center (from C to A, from D to A, and so on).

STRAIGHT STITCH

Straight Stitch is the most basic of all the embroidery stitches. This simple stitch can be worked in any direction and in any length to build any shape. Although it can be used alone, Straight Stitch is also the basis for many decorative stitches, such as Sheaf and Spider Web Stitches (see pages 30 and 31). You can make a flower (the basis for Spider Web Stitch) by working a series of Straight Stitches around a center point, (see above). Begin by drawing a circle and marking the center point.

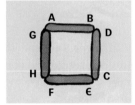

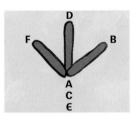

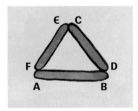

Ideas for how to use Straight Stitches

RUNNING STITCH

The most basic stitch, Running Stitch, is quick and easy. Running Stitch is used in quilting to hold several layers of fabric together. Begin by drawing a line.

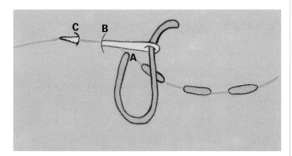

Come up at A, and insert your needle at B. Come up at C, and pull the needle through. Continue along the line, keeping the stitches evenly spaced. Once you feel comfortable, you can take several stitches at once.

Tip: To vary the look of Running Stitch, change the length of stitches in a pattern, such as short/short/long, short/short/long.

Short/short/long, short/short/long

SATIN STITCH

Use Satin Stitch for filling in any shape you can dream of. It is actually just a series of Straight Stitches packed closely together to form a mass of color. Satin Stitch, sometimes called Filling Stitch, looks incredibly easy to do, but it is actually one of the most challenging stitches to make perfectly neat. Begin by drawing a shape on the fabric.

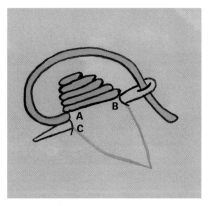

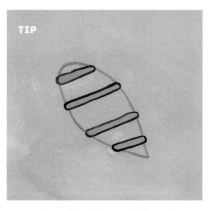

How to keep threads parallel in satin stitch

Beginning at one end of the shape, come up at A. Go down at B, then come up at C, right next to A. Continue in this way, packing the stitches closely together.

Tip: It's important, but sometimes tricky, to keep the stitches parallel and evenly spaced, so I like to work several stitches spaced evenly apart across the entire shape before I begin filling it in. To complete the area, I then fill in between the parallel stitches.

CROSS STITCH

Cross Stitch looks like the letter X. Traditionally, a series of Cross Stitches are worked to form a motif (design), but you can also use a single stitch by itself. Cross Stitch is often done on finely woven fabric with the stitches following the fabric weave, a technique that can be slightly tedious. Since I prefer stitching to be a happy and relaxing part of my day, I like to work Cross Stitch on gingham fabric (for projects, see pages 74–77). To work Cross Stitch on solid-color fabric, begin by drawing parallel lines about ½" apart.

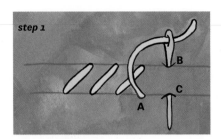

1. Come up at A on the lower line. Move your needle to the upper line at B, about ½" to the right of A. Go down at B and bring your needle up at C on the lower line directly below B. Pull the thread through.

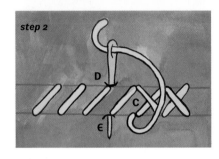

2. Continue to make a row of these slanted stitches between the lines. When you have completed the row, work from the end of the row in the opposite direction, making a series of slanted stitches that cross your first stitches, by inserting the needle at D and E.

STRAIGHT CROSS STITCH

Straight Cross Stitch looks like a plus (+) sign. It can be used in rows or singly to create texture. The goal is to make the stitch squarely set.

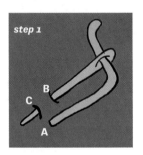

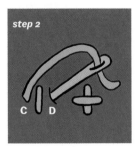

1. Come up at A. Go down at B (directly above A), then come up at C (to the left and at the mid-point between A and B).

2. Go down at D (directly opposite C) to complete the stitch.

BACKSTITCH

Backstitch is so named because each stitch is made by first stitching backward, then forward, resulting in a series of dashes placed close together. One of the most common stitches, it can be used for stems, lettering, and organic shapes. I used it for the lettering on the pillows on page 66, as well as in many other projects. Begin by drawing a line.

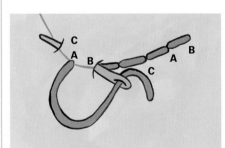

Come up at A, about ¼" from the end of the line. Insert your needle at B, about ¼" behind A, and come up at C, ¼" beyond A. Pull the stitch through. Continue in this fashion until your line is complete. To finish, stop stitching when you pull your needle through at B.

STEM STITCH

Another popular stitch, Stem Stitch (also called Outline Stitch) is useful for many purposes, such as stems, outlining, and lettering. It makes a thicker line than backstitch. If you pack the stitches very closely together, they fill in shapes beautifully and quickly. I used this stitch extensively for projects in this book. Begin by drawing a line.

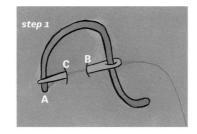

1. Come up at A at the beginning of the line. Take a backwards stitch from B to C (halfway between A and B), and pull the needle through, keeping the thread above the line of stitching.

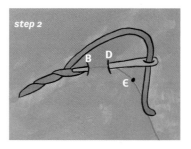

2. Take a stitch from D to B, keeping the thread above the line of stitching. You'll see that a heavy line of stitching develops as this new stitch overlaps the previous stitch. Make sure the thread always stays on one side of the line. To end, go down at E.

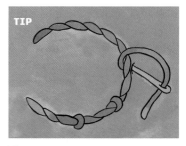

Tip: When you work around a curve, the threads sometimes fall down on the shape and you lose the clean line. To remedy this, work the stitches smaller than normal or work a small anchoring stitch over the Stem Stitch line to keep it in place. It will not show.

FERN STITCH

Fern Stitch looks like a lacy, stemmed fern and gives a delicate appearance to curving lines. For a more organic-looking design, vary the lengths and angles of the fronds. Begin by drawing a curving line.

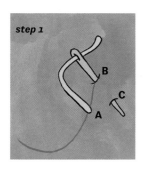

1. Come up at A about ½" from the beginning of the line. Insert the needle at B (the endpoint of the line), and come up at C, about ½" away from the line. Pull the needle through.

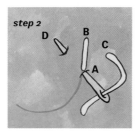

2. Insert the needle back at A on the line, and come up on the other side of the line at D. Pull the needle through.

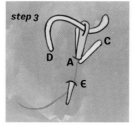

3. Insert the needle back at A on the line, and come up at E (about ½" down the line). Pull the needle through.

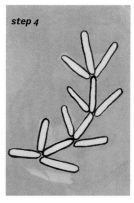

4. Continue Steps 1–3 until the line is filled in.

BLANKET STITCH

Blanket Stitch is a looped stitch (sometimes called Buttonhole Stitch). It is often worked along the edge of a blanket to create a decorative border that keeps the fabric from fraying. Before sewing machines were invented, buttonholes were created by packing this stitch closely together around a slit in the fabric. You can also use it to make a straight line of decorative stitches or stitch it in an organic fashion to form flowers (see page 136).

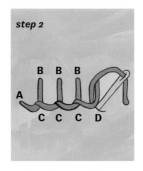

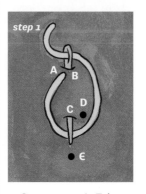

1. Come up at A. Insert your needle at B and come up at C, but do not pull the needle through until you wrap the thread under the needle. Then, pull the needle through to form a loop that resembles a J.

2. Continue working left to right to form a row of stitches. When your line is complete, go down at D, directly outside the loop, to anchor the stitch. Try to keep the stitches spaced evenly apart and the legs of the J the same length.

Tip: Alternatively, you can vary the length of the legs to create a decorative stitch, as shown.

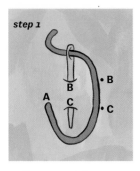

Blanket stitch is often worked over an edge of fabric as decoration or to prevent fraying. Begin with a knotted thread slightly in from the edge of the fabric (A). Insert the needle at B on the fabric itself, but C is "in the air" at the edge of the fabric. Make sure to loop the thread under the needle to cover the edge. To turn a corner, the first stitch should go over the straight edge; the second, over the corner; and the third, over the curved edge.

CHAIN STITCH

Chain Stitch is made by looping the thread around the needle. It actually looks like a chain. You can work it along a single line for outlines, lettering, or borders, or you can pack lines of chain stitch closely together to fill in shapes.

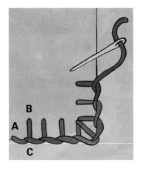

1. Come up at A. Take a stitch from B to C, but do not pull the needle through. Wrap the thread under the needle at C. Pull the needle through and a loop will form on top of the fabric. Continue by inserting your needle at D (inside the loop), then come up at E, again wrapping the yarn under the needle before you pull the needle through.

2. To end, insert your needle at F just outside the loop and pull to the back side to finish the stitch.

LAZY DAISY STITCH

The Lazy Daisy Stitch is a variation of Chain Stitch, in which each "chain" is worked separately. The traditional daisylike flower is created by working a series of Chain Stitches around a center point. A single lazy daisy makes a simple leaf.

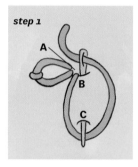

step 1

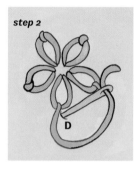

step 2

1. Come up at A. Insert your needle at B, and come up at C, but do not pull the needle through. Wrap the thread under the needle at C, then pull the needle through to form a loop.

2. End the stitch by inserting the needle at D to anchor the loop. Work additional stitches, keeping the start of each stitch close to the center and working the "petals" so that they radiate out.

FLY STITCH

The Fly Stitch (also known as Y Stitch) is similar to a Lazy Daisy Stitch but with an open end, which makes it look like a flying bird or the letter Y. Fly Stitch is useful for making the petals on flowers, like those on the napkins on page (120).

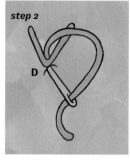

step 1

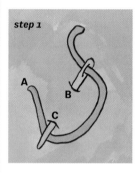

step 2

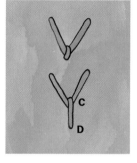

1. Come up at A. Insert your needle at B and come up at C. With the thread under the needle, pull the needle through to catch the thread.

2. Anchor the loop and thus finish the stitch by going down to the back of the fabric at D.

Alternate: To make the stitch look more like a Y, anchor the stitch by going down farther away from C at D.

HERRINGBONE STITCH

Very decorative, Herringbone Stitch looks like a series of x's worked on top of each other. I like to use this stitch for linear borders of decorative stitching (see page 53). Begin by drawing two parallel guidelines, about ½" apart.

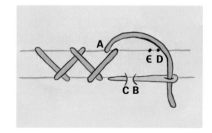

Working from left to right, bring your needle up at A on the upper guideline. Make a backward stitch at B and C on the lower guideline. Take a second backward stitch at D and E on the upper guideline. Continue in this way across your line. (Note: A and E are the same.)

FEATHER STITCH

Feather Stitch is extremely decorative, and it's fun to work, as well. It is made by looping the thread around the needle while moving the needle from one side of an imaginary line to the other side. When you work Feather Stitch, it feels rather like doing a dance with your needle: You swing your partner from side to side! You can work Feather Stitch very evenly and neatly, so that all the stitches form a rather geometric-looking design (see page 84) or you can vary the lengths and angles of the stitches (see page 64).

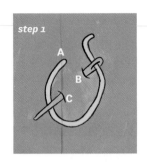

step 1

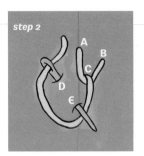

step 2

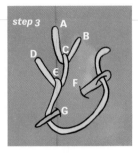

step 3

1. Come up at A. Take a stitch from B to C (just to the right of the line), leaving the needle in the fabric. Wrap the thread under the needle and pull the needle through.

2. Move the needle to the opposite side of the fabric and repeat the motion by going down at D and up at E (just to the left of the line), again catching the thread under the needle.

3. Move the needle back to the first side. Repeat the stitch and wrap from F to G. Continue until the line is filled in. Anchor the yarn on the outside of the stitch as you did for Chain Stitch.

FISHBONE STITCH

The Fishbone Stitch looks exactly like a fish vertebra after you have finished picking dinner clean. The threaded needle moves from side to side to create this clever stitch. You can work Fishbone Stitch closely together as I did on the Tuscan trees pillows (see page 63), or you can work it openly to form a lacier-looking leaf.

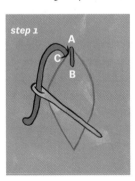

step 1

1. Come up at A, and make a straight stitch from A to B about ¼" long. Come up a C.

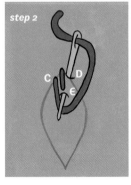

step 2

step 3

step 4

2. Go down at D, and come up at E directly below B keeping the thread below the needle.

3. Pull the needle through to catch the thread. Go down at F to anchor the loop.

4. Continue in this way until the entire shape is filled in.

FRENCH KNOT

French Knots are small globs of thread that make a textural bump on the surface of the fabric. They can be used en masse to create a bumpy surface to simulate curly hair or seeds in a flower. Used singly, they are the perfect center to a flower.

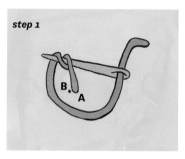

1. Come up at A. With your left hand (right hand, for lefties), wrap the thread twice around the needle.

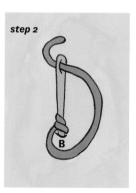

2. Rotate the needle toward the fabric, and insert the needle at B while tightly pulling on the wraps. Pull the needle to the back, and a knot will form on the surface.

Tip: Make sure B is not in the exact same place in the fabric as A, or the knot will disappear to the back side of the fabric.

BULLION KNOT

A Bullion Knot looks a lot like a caterpillar. The thread is wrapped around the needle in a corkscrew fashion to create a very textural, springy stitch. Use it to create single flowers or fur on animals. Once you master the technique (which I admit is a little tricky), vary the number of wraps to make an extra long, springy, loopy knot that looks like dreadlocks or the hair on a Puli dog.

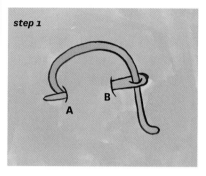

1. Come up at A, and take a stitch about ¼" long from B to A. Do not remove the needle from the fabric.

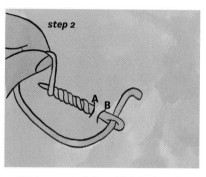

2. With your left hand (right hand, for lefties), wrap the thread around the needle seven times.

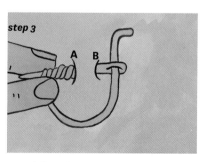

3. Holding the wrapped yarn on the needle with your pointer and thumb of your left hand, push the needle through the wraps and fabric, while pulling the knot toward B. The knot will flip toward B as you pull.

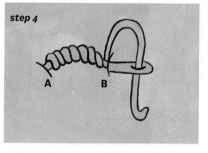

4. Using the point of the needle, arrange the wraps neatly. Go down at B to finish the stitch.

SHEAF STITCH

The Sheaf Stitch was named after the stacks of wheat that farmers used to pile and tie together in the fields at harvest, but it also looks like the torso of a finely shaped female. Sheaf Stitch looks nice in geometric arrangements and in straight lines of border treatments (see page 143).

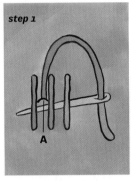 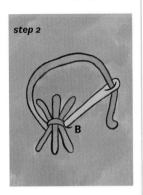

1. Make three straight stitches about ⅛" away from each other and about ½" long. Come up at A. Wrap the threaded needle around the three stitches twice, pulling tightly so that the stitches become bundled at the "waistline." Do not catch the fabric when wrapping the stitches.

2. Go down at B to finish.

Tip: To avoid catching the fabric when wrapping the stitches, work with the eye end of the needle toward the front as you wrap the thread around the sheaf.

LAID STITCH

The oddly named Laid Stitch attaches long, floating stitches to fabric with smaller Cross Stitches in contrasting colors. Laid Stitch looks like a garden trellis or graph paper, depending on the direction in which it is worked. It can be done in squares, diamonds, or any organic shape. It fills in large spaces quickly with decorative appeal (see page 121).

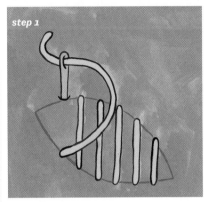 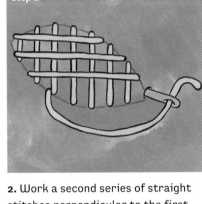

1. Work a series of straight stitches, evenly spaced to fill in the desired shape.

2. Work a second series of straight stitches perpendicular to the first. The resulting set of long stitches will be loose and floppy and resemble a plaid.

3. With a second color, work two diagonal stitches at each intersection of the threads to anchor them to the fabric (see Cross Stitch on page 24).

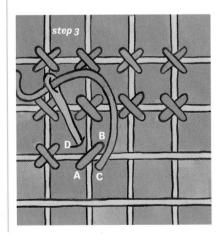

SPIDER WEB STITCH

If you learned to weave when you were young, you'll find Spider Web Stitch lots of fun. I used it for the polka dots on page 110 and the flower centers on page 137. Leave the spokes half-woven to make a flower or sun. Try using different thread colors to create multi-colored webs. You can work Spider Web Stitch over any odd number of "spokes."

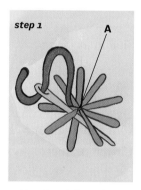

step 1

A

step 2

1. Use Straight Stitch to work nine radiating "spokes" around a center point. (For Straight Stitch, see page 22.) Using a blunt-tipped needle, come up at A in the center of the spokes.

2. Weave over and under every other spoke, spiraling outward until the entire shape is filled. Pack the stitches down as the spokes fill up to create a filled-in weaving. End by drawing the yarn through to the back side under a spoke.

Tip: Weave with the eye end of the needle toward the front if you don't have a blunt-tipped needle. Note that as you weave and pack down the yarn, the spokes disappear under the weaving.

NEEDLEWEAVING

Needleweaving is very similar to Spider Web Stitch and just as much fun to do. You actually create a small piece of floating fabric as you weave over two or more threads on a fabric base. Two threads make an interesting sculptural petal or leaf for a flower (see page 138). By weaving over irregularly spaced base threads, you can create large leaves. You can even create odd shapes, like a skirt or pants, using this technique. If you vary the tension of the threads, weaving more loosely toward the center of the anchor threads, you can create an oval-shaped piece of fabric that resembles a petal or a leaf. I used needleweaving to create the sculptural, natural-shaped leaves on page 94.

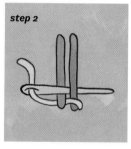

step 1

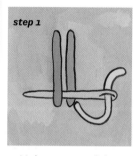

step 2

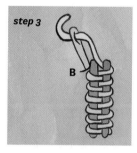

step 3

B

1. Make two straight stitches the same length, spaced about ⅛ " apart. Using a blunt-tipped needle, come up at A and go over the first base thread and under the second.

2. Turn the needle in the opposite direction and go over the first thread and under the second thread.

3. Continue in this manner until both base threads are completely filled. Pack down the threads with the back end of the needle as you fill the base threads. End by going down at B.

Tip: Weave with the eye end of the needle at the front if you do not have a blunt-tipped needle. The base threads become hidden as you pack in the weaving.

A Stitched Page Marker

It's probably been a few years since you made your mom a bookmark, but it's never too late to rekindle those grade-school skills. Bookmarks are the perfect project for trying out new stitches and making a functional gift at the same time — perfect to mail to a faraway relative you've been thinking about or to include in a book you're passing on to a friend.

Made with soft, colored felt, my bookmarks remind me of something I might be lucky enough to find in a Victorian-era novel at a used-book store. Felt is the perfect fabric, because you can cut it down to size without having to finish the edges — felted cloth doesn't fray.

Follow the formula on the facing page, if you wish, or let go and use your own inventive cleverness to modify my designs and create your own. Making a bookmark is a great way to try out your new stitches. It's something you can complete in an evening with a feeling of accomplishment and satisfaction. Consider using randomly placed French Knots, flowers, sun motifs, even stripes and plaids. Edge your bookmark with Blanket or Running Stitch. Make them simple or complicated — it's up to you.

FINISHED SIZE: 1½" x 6"

FABRIC

Small pieces of wool felt

THREAD

Odds and ends of 3-ply Persian wool or 6-strand cotton embroidery floss in a variety of pretty colors

NOTIONS

Size 20 chenille needle

STITCHES

Backstitch (page 24)

Bullion Stitch (page 29)

Feather Stitch (page 28)

Fern Stitch (page 25)

Fly Stitch (page 27)

Herringbone Stitch (page 27)

Lazy Daisy (page 27)

Stem Stitch (page 25)

Running Stitch (page 23)

Spider Web Stitch (page 31)

Straight Stitch (page 22)

Straight Cross Stitch (page 24)

PREPARING THE FABRIC

1. Using a see-through ruler and a water-soluble or child's washable marker, measure and draw a rectangle 1½" × 6" on a piece of wool felt. Cut along the lines. (Cut several at once, for future projects.)

2. Using the same marker, draw a line lengthwise down the center of the rectangle. If you're working a centered motif, mark the center of the rectangle widthwise, as well.

A DESIGN WITHOUT A CENTRAL MOTIF

3. Stitch along the lengthwise line, beginning and ending ¼" from the ends of the bookmark, using any one of the following:

- Fern Stitch
- Feather Stitch
- Herringbone Stitch
- Running Stitch

For flower buds, if desired, work French Knots or Bullion Stitch at the ends of the legs of the Fern or Feather Stitches. Alternate Running Stitches with French Knots or Straight Cross Stitches with French Knots at their centers.

A DESIGN WITH A CENTRAL MOTIF

4. Work one of the following designs at the center mark:

- Lazy Daisy with a French Knot center
- Spider Web center with Fly Stitch "petals"
- Satin Stitch center with Straight Stitch "rays" (a sun)

5. Stitching along the lengthwise line you drew in step 2, and beginning and ending ¼" from the ends of the bookmark, work any one of the following up to the central motif:

- Stem Stitch
- Backstitch
- Running Stitch
- Fern Stitch

FINISHING THE BOOKMARK

6. Remove the marker lines with a spritz of water. Use a steam iron to even out the stitching.

finding inspiration

I'm passionate about embroidery because I see it not only as a fun hobby but as a very personal and creative form of art. At first, you may not feel comfortable designing your projects. If that's where you are, by all means just enjoy yourself and follow my instructions for the projects in this book to the letter. But as you gain confidence, you'll probably be itching to test your innate design talents and discover that they are just waiting to explode.

I often hear people say, "Oh, I'm just not creative. I could never do what you do." But I believe that designing needlework, painting a picture, knitting a sweater, decorating your home, or cooking a good meal are all creative activities. Once you develop your creative skills, in no matter what area, you can translate them as you work in another discipline. You'll soon find yourself producing beautiful items and leading a more artistic life.

Try this to begin: Think of something you like best in this world, something so special that you would enjoy simplifying and translating it into a design that you could immortalize in a piece of stitchery. If you're stuck for an idea, how about your own home? Or, comb through old postcards and souvenirs of a special trip, perhaps to the Eiffel Tower, Buckingham Palace, or the Empire State Building. See Inspirations to Explore (facing page) to get you thinking; don't hesitate to add more.

MILES OF FILES

The next step in the design process is to collect images. Clip pictures from discarded magazines, newspapers, old books, and postcards. I like to take digital photos, which I save on my computer as a resource. Put everything you collect into an idea file. I enjoy tacking my favorites up on the wall so I can muse about them and absorb their beauty. I'm always looking for new ideas that will stimulate me when I move on to the next project.

Keep a sketchbook. I have piles of sketchbooks that I've been filling for years. They aren't fancy. It's fun to look through my old sketchbooks and remember particular museum visits, dinners, and shopping expeditions. It makes me think back to why I was attracted to something particular in the first place and how my sketching and designing has changed and improved over the years.

My life is as chaotic as yours, and my messy basement studio is where I pile up my ideas as they come in. The piles keep growing, sometimes to seemingly unmanageable levels, but I let them accumulate. I know that when I need to propose a new book or design, all I have to do is go to my collection and an idea will come. I keep my space private and don't allow my family to use it. If you have only a closet and a bulletin board to devote to your own idea file, that will be room enough.

Inspirations to Explore

- My pets (cats, dogs, birds, iguanas, hamsters, fish)
- Native plants and mushrooms
- Birds and butterflies
- Sunsets and clouds
- Flowers and gardens
- History
- Architecture
- Antiques
- Ceramics
- Geometric shapes
- Typefaces and lettering
- Books and libraries
- Comic books
- A particular era in time (like the '50s)
- Fashion
- Pop culture
- Music
- Kids
- Circus
- Other cultures

field trips

Visit museums for inspiration. They don't have to be the fanciest museums in the country: The local historical society will do! Museums give you a glimpse into the past or a different culture. Let beautiful objects and paintings fuel your ideas. Take along a little sketchbook and pencil to make small, representational drawings of ideas you like. Note the color combinations that you're drawn to in a painting or a piece of pottery. Collect museum postcards.

Don't forget your local library, which is jam-packed with books full of photos and illustrations. Best of all, it's free. The magazine you can't afford may be at your local library. Check out your favorite books and explore them at home. Add to your idea file by copying ideas into your sketchbook. All that you observe will put a new spin on your designing. This isn't copying: It's called *inspiration*, and every artist has his or her own favorite sources.

your first design

have on hand

Photograph of
  a building

Pencil and eraser

Tracing paper

Felt-tipped pen

See-through ruler

Here's how I translated a photograph of my home into a simple hand-stitched pillow.

1. My photo wasn't perfect, just representational enough that I could glean the basic structure. Any junk in the yard (like an old wheelbarrow) can be creatively edited out. I used a photocopier to increase the image to the size I wanted for the finished project.

step 1

2. I laid a piece of tracing paper over the image and traced the basic outline with pencil. I like using a see-through ruler so I can get straight lines. With the highlights of the building covered, I added a few details.

3. I lifted the tracing paper off the picture and thought about what it would be like to stitch over the lines I'd drawn, which stitches I could use, and the colors I might choose. I then placed another piece of tracing paper over my drawing, and redrew the house. I simplified it because I knew I wouldn't want to stitch the little details.

4. For my final version, I made the house squarer than it really is. I added some smoke and an imaginary walk. I then transferred the design to the fabric using the photocopy method (see page 19).

step 2

step 3

step 4

5. I chose the stitches as I went along. If I didn't like the way one looked, I ripped it out and tried another. Whenever I'm stitching, I'm also thinking of new ideas for future projects.

6. I made the finished stitchery into a pillow with multi-color pompoms at the corners.

who's afraid of color?

Every once in a while I have a nightmare: I dream I am color blind. I wake up startled and disturbed that I might have to live a life without seeing color. Then I turn on my bedside lamp and look at the brightly painted shade and am relieved that I can still see all the beautiful, vibrant shades I love. Color fills me with joy. Color also gives me endless, delightful hours of experimentation and learning — and I will never be done learning about color.

Color is extremely personal. My daughter, Julia, frequently asks me what my favorite color is. Her standard answer is "pink"; my standard answer is "green," because it comes in so many different shades, from the chartreuse of the opening leaves in spring, to the electric shades of velvety moss on the forest floor, to the deep evergreens and cedars of coastal Maine, to the faded grey greens of the spent leaves at the end of summer in my garden. Sometimes I throw her a curve and say "orange" or "blue," but always I tell her there's no color I don't like or appreciate.

After decades of observing colors, I realize it is the interplay and relationship of colors that hold the most fascination for me. Two objects of different colors are usually more appealing than one. Throw in a few more colors and I am a happy camper.

The photos on the facing page illustrate a simple way to observe how colors work together. I purchased three Gerbera daisies — orange, yellow, and pink — and laid each one on several different-colored pieces of fabric. Where the daisy and the fabric are very close in shade (for example, the pink daisy on the orange fabric), the colors look nice together, but there isn't a lot of excitement or interest in the combination. But look at the same pink daisy on the periwinkle blue fabric. This combination is better, but still not wild. Now, look at that same pink daisy on the bright green fabric. All of a sudden, your brain is stimulated and happy — the colors bounce against each other. Look at each of the other combinations and note how you react to each. Which do you like the best? Which does nothing for your senses? Notice how with some combinations the flower fades away, because there's not enough difference in the *shades* (the color) or the *tones* (the darkness or lightness of the color), whereas in others the effect is exciting and vibrant.

This is how I work with color everyday. I get new ideas for color combinations by laying fabrics and yarns against each other to see how they interact. When I'm planning a project, I lay the yarn I'm going to stitch with on top of my ground fabric. Do the colors pop and vibrate against each other? Is there enough difference in their lightness or darkness to make my stitching stand out and be noticed? If I'm going to take time to handstitch something, I want it to be a beautiful, cheerful object when it's completed.

Three Gerbera daisies, placed on six different-colored fabrics demonstrate how color interactions create completely different effects.

working with color

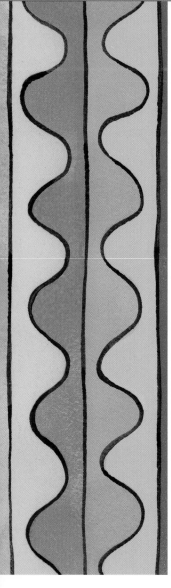

You've got your favorite colors and color combinations, and you love to be surrounded by them, but try to break out of your box and use these favorites with other, more off-beat shades. Read on to stretch your color boundaries.

OBSERVE NATURE

On a sunny morning, grab a notebook and a basket and head for the woods, the park, or your garden. Pick up leaves, acorns, stones, and flowers. Spread them out and write down what colors you see in each object. Observe like a child. You'll see that nature doesn't make something in only one shade; a single leaf or rock boasts many colors. Return to your little pile again at noon. You'll notice that the colors look different now. The sun has shifted, and light is reflected off the objects differently, making colors more washed out. Write down your observations. Go back again about a half hour before sunset. You'll notice that the colors are once again different with the changed angle of light making them deeper, more shadowy, and more interesting.

STUDY MAGAZINES

Subscribe to lushly photographed publications such as *National Geographic* or garden design magazines, which offer a wealth of inspiration about the workings of natural colors. Tear out pictures with color combinations that especially appeal to you.

MUSEUM HOPPING

Spend a day at a museum. Whenever I feel culturally starved and visually lost, it takes only a bit of browsing through a museum or art gallery to lift my spirits and fuel my designing ways. If you've never taken time to do this before, and your only memories are of being totally bored on grade school trips to museums, try again. Bring your trusty sketchbook and some colored pencils. Walk through the Italian Renaissance, float through the French Impressionists, and succumb to mid-20th century modernists. Observe how color is used and combined in the paintings. Write down and sketch what you observe. From afar something may look blue, but move in closer and inspect the painting. That blue you saw from afar, may be made up of blues, greens, greys, reds, and yellows. Looking at art closely gives you fascinating insights into how artists work with color, which can help you learn how to work with it successfully, too.

THINK LIKE AN ARTIST

Van Gogh said of his painting *Starry Night,* "I absolutely want to paint a starry sky. It often seems to me that the night is still more richly colored than the day, having hues of the most intense violets, blues, and greens. If only you pay attention to it, you will see that certain stars are citron-yellow, others have a pink glow or a green, blue and forget-me-not brilliance.

And without my expatiating on this theme, it will be clear that putting little white dots on a blue-black surface is not enough." (Vincent Van Gogh, *Art, Life, and Letters,* by Bernard Zurcher, Thunder Bay Press, 1985.) Van Gogh was a color genius. Purchase postcards of your favorite artist's work. Study them and absorb the colors and color combinations and learn from the artist's work.

WAKE UP AND SMELL THE COFFEE!

Perhaps you don't have time to tiptoe through nature and you live nowhere near a major city museum. That's no excuse. Keep your eyes open; notice and write down combinations that appeal to you. Look at kids' books: Children's book illustrators use color fabulously. Rifle through your pantry and examine the packaging of your favorite foods. Do you buy that spaghetti because you like the colors on the box? Once you start observing, you'll be securely hooked on color.

LEARN ABOUT THE COLOR WHEEL

Purchase a color wheel (see at right) and use it as a guide. Developed by Sir Isaac Newton in 1666, the color wheel is made up of 12 slices. When you combine colors that are opposite (or almost so) on the wheel, you start to get some visual excitement. Called *complementary colors,* these are some of the most fun combinations to play with. Nature offers many shocking complementary combinations. For instance, the orange-red soil of the Desert Southwest vibrates against the deep turquoise sky. New England's autumn copper, orange, and yellow leaves sparkle against blue skies. A brilliant red male cardinal perches in a deep green rose bush.

You may decide that complementary color combinations aren't for you. Your tastes fall toward calmer combinations of blue with blue-green or red with orange. Pick shades that are next to each other on the color wheel. To make your stitched design show up when using colors that are close to each other on the wheel, make one of colors much darker than the other. (See Naturally Inspired on page 62.) For a very subtle, tone-on-tone look, stitch with the same color as your ground fabric. The subtle result is sophisticated, like a jacquard tablecloth.

GETTING OUT OF THE RUT

Whichever color path you follow for your first projects, keep stretching your boundaries as your skills progress. Whether you use nature, art, or the color wheel as your guide, it is exhilarating to work with color — you never know where the next idea will come from or what you will create. With each project, choose new colors for your stitching combinations. You'll learn a little and be lifted right out of that color rut.

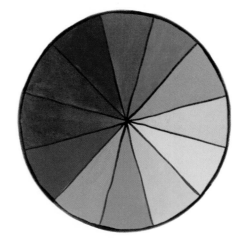

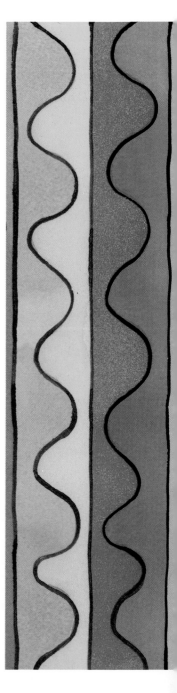

Pillows with Personality

Pillows are like earrings: They add the crowning touch to a couch, chair, or bed. They also bring personality to a tired décor. They can be richly colorful and jewel-like, classic and comfortable, avant-garde and dashing, or cozy and calm. You can quickly change an entire room's design focus simply by changing the pillows on your couch. And if the pillows are hand-stitched, so much the better. They make a statement that this home is happy and comfortable, and full of love.

Pillows are the perfect first project for a new stitcher (or for someone who hasn't stitched in awhile), and they don't need to be boring. They don't take much fabric, thread, or time. Even if you've never sewn a seam in your life and you don't have a sewing machine, you can make a pillow. Simply sew two squares of fabric together, turn the whole thing right side out, and voilà — a cozy, comfortable pillow.

If you're inspired, pull out all the stops and add pompoms and tassels. Decorate every chair in your house with a hand-stitched pillow. When you're done with your own home, start making pillows for friends. Jump in with both feet and start stitching — and re-decorating!

pillow talk

The first step in pillow-making is to prepare the fabric, both backs and fronts. It's best to stitch the design on the ground fabric *before* you assemble the pillow, so the back isn't in your way when you're stitching.

Each set of instructions in this book gives a *finished* pillow size, which is the size after assembly. The *cutting* size of each pillow front allows for a ½" seam and the use of an embroidery hoop, if needed. It is 3" larger, vertically and horizontally, than the finished pillow size.

LET'S GET IT STRAIGHT

It's important to ensure that your fabric is straight and lines up properly once you've completed the pillow. Before you cut, therefore, you need to find the straight (or even) grain of the fabric — the direction in which the individual

threads that make up the fabric are woven. Gently pull on a thread perpendicular to the *selvedge* (the tightly woven side edge) until the whole length comes out of the fabric. As you tease the thread along, the fabric will gather up a bit. If it breaks, just pull a thread next to it. The space created by the pulled thread is your cutting guideline for a perfect straight edge.

You can also rip many fabrics along the straight grain. Snip into the piece 2" from a straight edge along a thread. Grasp the fabric on each side of the cut, and pull each side in the opposite direction until the fabric begins to tear. Small puckered threads sometimes distort torn edges, but you can usually smooth these out with a steam iron. With a see-through ruler, measure for the other two sides of the pillow, using the cut edge and selvedges as reference points.

WORKING WITH SCAVENGED FABRICS

To salvage squared-up pieces from a vintage garment, cut along the seams to free the largest areas of the fabric. Determine the straight grain by pulling a loose thread and proceeding as described above. For knitted pieces, unravel a row of knitting by pulling a thread crosswise. You can cut felted fabrics (especially felted knits) any way you want. The felt has become a mass unto itself, stable and easy to sew or cut in any direction.

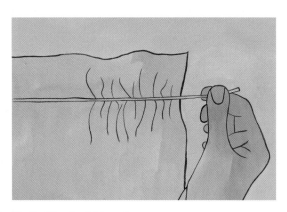

Finding the straight grain

*i*f you find your stitches are distorting the ground fabric so much that blocking won't fix them, an embroidery hoop is for you. An embroidery hoop keeps the ground fabric of your stitchery taut so that the stitches you make are even. It can be especially helpful when you're just learning to stitch and feeling a little anxious about it, which can cause you to stitch too tightly. But even if you're not a beginner, your personality may influence whether or not you prefer using a hoop. If you're someone who enjoys getting each detail correct, chances are that you'll like one. On the other hand, if you're more casual, then you'll probably be making looser stitches and not want to be encumbered by a hoop.

You usually don't need a hoop if you're stitching on stiff or heavy fabric, such as recycled wools, coating fabrics, heavy linens, or felt, because you're less likely to pull the stitches too tightly and distort these fabrics. I like to use an embroidery hoop when I'm working on finer ground fabrics, such as cotton gingham, as well as on many linen fabrics that will be heavily decorated with stitches. As your skills increase, you'll be able to judge when you need one. Using common sense and relaxing while you stitch are the best ways to keep your work from puckering.

How to use a hoop. Separate the two pieces by loosening the screw on the outer hoop. Lay the smaller hoop (the one without the screw) down on your lap. Place the fabric so that the section to be stitched is centered on the hoop. Lay the larger hoop (the one with the screw) over the smaller one and push down, sandwiching the fabric between the two pieces. Tighten the screw. Pull the fabric down evenly around the hoop to make the fabric taut, like a drum.

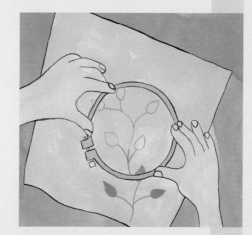

When you finish stitching an area, remove the hoop and reposition it on another part of the design. Don't leave your fabric in the hoop for extremely long periods of time or the fabric may become permanently distorted.

To Hoop or Hoop?

Honey, I Shrunk the Blanket . . .

Who hasn't shrunken a wool sweater by misplacing it in the wrong load of wash and ending up with an outfit just right for your child's teddy bear. But you can intentionally shrink wool fabric with wonderful results, and then it is called *felting*. Felted wool makes a fabulous ground fabric, and I used it for many of the projects in this book.

Felting is another step toward creating your very own designer fabric. Make sure that the garment or fabric you choose to felt is at least 80 percent wool and hasn't been treated. (If it's labeled "superwash," the wool fiber has been chemically treated *not* to felt.) If the fabric is fluffy and hairy, it will felt well. Wool blankets are great to felt: They often need only one wash cycle for great results. This is because they've already been felted at the factory just enough to make them thicker and warmer. Women's dressy angora and wool sweaters also felt beautifully, and you may be able to find them in lots of nice colors. The sky's the limit, and your washing machine does all the work! Have fun and experiment. Here's how to do it:

1. Throw the fabric, blanket, or sweater in the washing machine with your normal laundry detergent and some washing soda if you have it. Set the machine for a hot wash and a cold rinse, and walk away. The felting works best if the load is at least half full, so add other items for friction. Avoid adding towels, however, because if those toweling fibers shed, they'll become permanently embedded in the felt.

2. When the cycle is complete, come back and inspect the fabric. If it hasn't felted enough, run the machine again. Some wool fabrics need to be felted several times before they are pleasing, though some never shrink. Nicely felted fabric should be thicker and denser than when you began. When you examine it, you shouldn't be able to see the weave or knit structure any longer. The surface should be hairy, with tangled fibers.

Warning: Felting can become addictive! I have a friend who broke her washing machine by felting too many heavy things.

putting it all together

After you've completed the stitchery and blocked your piece (for blocking, see page 21), you need to trim the pillow front to 1" larger than the desired finished size, to allow for a ½" seam all around. In many projects, it's very important to keep your design centered, so you will probably need to trim around all four sides. For instance, if you are making a 14" square pillow, measure 7½" out from the center to each edge to get a 15" square, then cut off the excess on each edge; this will keep your design at the exact center.

BACKS THAT STAND UP TO THEIR FRONTS

I like to back all my pillows with beautiful fabrics that contrast with the embroidered fronts. Finding a lovely print on the back of a hand-embroidered pillow is a nice surprise! And it's fun to hunt for colorful, patterned remnants to use as backings for stitched pillows. When you're cleaning out closets and discarding old clothes, save some of the prettier fabrics for pillow backings.

   I use two different methods for backing my pillows: a neat flap for a removable pillow insert or a non-removable style, which isn't as elegant or useful but is easier to make.

When measuring for the final trim, it's important to keep designs like the one on the pillow at the right carefully centered on the fabric.

PILLOW BACK WITH A FLAP

The flap-style pillow back makes it easy to quickly remove the pillow cover for laundering.

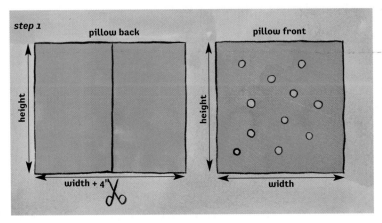

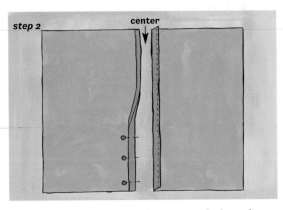

1. Using the completed piece as a guide, measure and cut fabric for the pillow back to the same *height* as the trimmed front (including the seam allowance). Measure and cut it 3" *wider* than the trimmed pillow front. Fold the piece in half widthwise, and cut along the fold line. (See below for common sizes.)

2. Lay the two pillow back pieces side-by-side, right side down. Fold the center edges under ½" to the wrong side and press. Fold under ½" again, press, and hand- or machine-stitch a hem in place along fold.

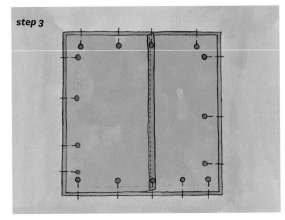

3. Lay the trimmed, embroidered piece right-side up on a table. Place one of the backing pieces on top of embroidery with its right side facing the stitchery, outer edges matching, and hemmed edge in center. Pin. Place other piece right-side down, facing the embroidery, also with outer edges matching and hemmed edge in the center. The pieces will overlap in the middle.

CUTTING SIZES FOR FLAPPED-BACK PILLOW

FINISHED PILLOW SIZE	PILLOW FRONT (INC. SEAM ALLOWANCE)	PILLOW BACK (CUT 2)
12" square	13" x 13"	13" x 8"
14" square	15" x 15"	15" x 9"
16" square	17" x 17"	17" x 10"
18" square	19" x 19"	19" x 11"
20" square	21" x 21"	21" x 12"
12" x 18"	13" x 19"	13" x 11"

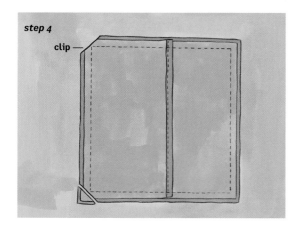

step 4

clip

4. Sew around all four sides of pillow, taking up a ½" seam allowance. For neater corners, clip all four diagonally to remove excess fabric. Turn pillow right-side out. Use a knitting needle or a capped pen to push out corners of pillow from inside. Press to flatten seams. Insert pillow form.

NON-REMOVABLE PILLOW CONSTRUCTION

Lay trimmed, embroidered piece right-side up on a table. Cut pillow-back fabric exactly the same size. With right sides together, pin the two pieces together. Sew around pillow, taking up a ½" seam allowance. Leave 7" unstitched, centered on one edge of pillow. Trim corners to remove excess fabric and make turning easier. Turn pillow right-side out. Use a knitting needle or capped pen to push out corners. Press to flatten seams. Stuff with filling or a pillow form, and sew opening closed using Whip Stitch.

THE STUFF PILLOWS ARE MADE OF

Consider investing in a good down or feather-and-down insert for your hand-stitched pillow — it will last a lifetime. The embroidered cover may wear out first, but when it does, you can enjoy making a new one for the old down insert.

The chart below shows the dimensions of the most common pillow inserts. Plan your embroidered pieces to fit the inserts that are available. If your pillow cover is larger than your insert, however, you can use loose stuffing to fill up the corners. If the pillow comes out smaller than the insert, creatively jam the insert in: It will just be a little fatter.

If you need to make an odd-size pillow, follow the instructions for a non-removable pillow. Stuff it with loose stuffing, which comes in cotton, polyester, or wool, and is available at most craft and sewing stores. Whipstitch the edges closed.

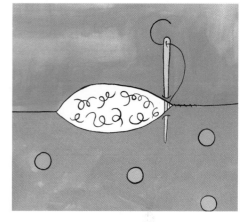

Whipstitching the edges closed

COMMON PILLOW INSERT SIZES	
Decorative throw pillows	12", 14", 16", 18", 20", 26", and 30" square
Rectangular pillows	12" x 16", 12" x 18", 16" x 20" (often called a travel pillow)
Bed pillows	20" x 26" (Standard), 20" x 30" (Queen), 20" x 36" (King)

Super-Simple Striped Pillows

These delightfully simple striped pillows are the perfect choice for your first project — and perfect for snuggling with on winter evenings while reading or stitching in front of a glowing fire. They require very little stitching and the finished look is bold. I felted and dyed the fabrics for the red and orange pillows, both thrift shop finds. (For felting, see page 46; for dyeing, see page 14.) I used worsted-weight wool knitting yarn so that my stitches could be thicker and quicker than those done with traditional embroidery threads. I chose pretty silk and cotton prints to back the pillows, since felted wool would have been too heavy to use for both front and back when turning the pillow inside out to finish it. Tassels at each corner made with the leftover worsted-weight wool knitting yarn give this easy-to-make trio a very festive look.

Throughout history, tassels have led a very decorative and celebratory life. You'll find them attached to fancy curtains and pillows in historic homes. They grace graduation caps every June. In the Andes, llamas wear red tassels on their ears, because the tassels are thought to increase fertility.

The instructions given here make a basic, no-frills tassel. Once you've made a few, you may develop your own tasseled art form. Tassels use lots of yarn, so you'll soon discover that knitting yarns are a less expensive option than embroidery threads. You'll need about 12 yards of yarn for each tassel, a small piece of cardboard from a corrugated box, cellophane tape, and sharp scissors. Here's how to proceed:

1. For a 4" tassel, cut two pieces of cardboard 3" x 4". Holding the two pieces of cardboard, wrap cellophane packing tape around them, fastening the two pieces together and covering all the edges of the cardboard with tape. (This makes it easy to slide the yarn off the cardboard in step 4.)

2. Cut two pieces of yarn (the same yarn you are using for the tassels or a stronger yarn, if the tassel yarn is loosely twisted) 10" long. Set these pieces aside.

3. Tightly wrap the yarn around the cardboard, layering it as shown in the illustration below. The more yarn you wrap, the thicker and denser the tassel will be: 60 wraps makes a nice tassel. Cut the end of the yarn.

Tip: You can speed this process by drawing yarn from two skeins of yarn at once. You wrap the cardboard only half as many times to get the same thickness!

4. Thread one 10" length of yarn under the bundle of yarn at one end of the cardboard, and tie a double knot, leaving the ends long for attaching the tassel to the project. Slide the yarn off the cardboard. With sharp scissors, cut through the loops at the free (untied) end of the bundle.

5. Wrap the second 10" piece of yarn snugly around the bundle about 1" below the tie, and tie a knot. Flip the tassel over and tie a second knot. Thread these ends through a tapestry needle, and draw both ends to the inside of the tassel. Trim the ends to neaten.

6. Use the loose ends at the top of the tassel to attach it by threading each end through a needle separately and using the needle to draw the end to the inside of the pillow. Tie the two ends on the inside to secure.

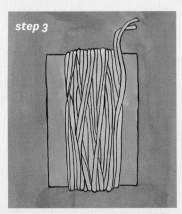

step 3

step 4

step 5

herringbone stitch pillow

I made this pillow from a remnant of coating fabric.

FINISHED SIZE: 14" x 14"

FABRICS

⅝ yard wool fabric, for pillow front

½ yard print cotton or silk fabric, for pillow back

THREAD

Any blue worsted-weight wool knitting yarn

I used Nashua Handknits Julia (50% wool/25% alpaca/ 25% mohair), 93 yd (85 m)/1.75 oz (50 gm) skeins: one skein in Electric Blue/3983.

NOTIONS

Size 18 chenille needle

14" square pillow insert (preferably down)

STITCHES

Herringbone Stitch
(page 27)

PREPARING THE PILLOW FRONT AND BACK

1. Measure and cut a 17" square from the wool for the pillow front (see page 44).
2. Measure and cut pillow back fabric for either a non-removable cover or a flapped back opening for a 14" square pillow (see page 48). Set pillow back aside.
3. Referring to diagram on page 185, use a see-through ruler and a water-soluble or child's washable marker to draw three parallel, ½" wide stripes, 3¼" apart and centered on the fabric. These lines mark the width of your Herringbone Stitches.

STITCHING THE DESIGN

4. Beginning 1" in from the edge of the fabric, work Herringbone Stitch between the paired guidelines.

FINISHING THE PILLOW

5. Neaten thread ends by trimming to ¼"; remove all marking lines. Block and press pillow front (see page 21). Keeping middle Herringbone stripe centered, trim front to 15" square.
6. With right sides facing, stitch front and back together, taking a ½" seam allowance (see pages 48–49) for backing you chose).
7. Using the wool yarn, make four tassels (see page 52). Attach one tassel at each of the four corners, using the pair of long tails at the top of the tassel as ties.
8. Stuff with pillow insert.

marking wool fabric

Because of its nap, you may have some difficulty getting good, clear marks on wool. I like to use a child's washable marker for this. Be patient and take it slowly so that the color penetrates the fabric.

running stitch pillow

The fabric for the orange pillow came from a pale pink blanket that I purchased for two dollars at a local thrift store.

FINISHED SIZE: 14" x 14"

FABRICS

⅝ yard recycled blanket or coating, dyed orange, for pillow front

½ yard of print linen or cotton fabric, for pillow back

THREAD

Any blue worsted-weight wool knitting yarn

I used Nashua Handknits Julia (50% wool/25% alpaca/ 25% mohair), 93 yd (85 m)/1.75 oz (50 gm) skeins: one skein in Electric Blue/3983.

NOTIONS

Size 18 chenille needle

14" square pillow insert (preferably down)

STITCHES

Running Stitch
(page 23)

PREPARING THE PILLOW FRONT AND BACK

1. Measure and cut a 17" square from the wool for the pillow front (see page 44).
2. Measure and cut the pillow back fabric for either a non-removable cover or a flapped back opening for a 14" square pillow (see page 48). Set pillow back aside.
3. Referring to the diagram on page 185, use a see-through ruler and a water-soluble or child's washable marker to draw seven stitching guidelines, spaced 2" apart, with the middle one centered on the fabric.

STITCHING THE DESIGN

4. Using a doubled thread, work Running Stitches, approximately ⅜" long, along the length of the guidelines, beginning about 1" in from the edge of the fabric.
5. Continue until all seven guidelines have been stitched.

FINISHING THE PILLOW

6. Neaten the thread ends by trimming to ¼", and remove all marking lines. Block and press the pillow front (see page 21).
7. Keeping the middle line of stitching centered, trim the pillow front to 15" square.
8. With right sides facing, stitch the front and back together, taking a ½" seam allowance and following the instructions on pages 48–49) for the type of backing you chose.
9. Make four tassels from the wool yarn (see page 52). Using the pair of long tails at the top of the tassels as ties, attach one tassel at each of the four corners.
10. Stuff with pillow insert.

chain stitch pillow

I felted and dyed a white wool, ribbed pullover sweater for the fabric for this pillow.

FINISHED SIZE: 14" x 14"

FABRICS

Sweater, felted and dyed red, or ⅝ yard red coating fabric, machine washed to slightly felt it, for pillow front

½ yard of print cotton or silk fabric, for pillow back

THREAD

Any gold and green worsted-weight wool knitting yarns

I used Nashua Handknits Julia (50% wool/25% alpaca/25% mohair), 93 yd (85 m)/1.75 oz (50 gm) skeins: one skein each in Chartreuse/3961 and Gold/2163.

NOTIONS

Size 18 chenille needle

14" square pillow insert (preferably down)

STITCHES

Chain Stitch
(page 26)

PREPARING THE PILLOW FRONT AND BACK

1. Measure and cut a 17" square from the wool for the pillow front (see page 44).
2. Measure and cut the pillow back fabric for either a non-removable cover or a flapped back opening for a 14" square pillow (see page 48). Set pillow back aside.
3. Referring to the diagram on page 186, use a see-through ruler and a water-soluble or child's washable marker to draw nine stitching guidelines, spaced 1½" apart, with the middle one centered on the fabric.

STITCHING THE DESIGN

4. Using the gold yarn, and beginning about 1" in from the edge, work Chain Stitch along one of your guidelines to within 1" of the opposite edge. Space your stitches about ⅜" away from each other.
5. Continue working Chain Stitch along the guidelines, alternating lines of chartreuse and gold, until all the lines are covered.

FINISHING THE PILLOW

6. Neaten the thread ends by trimming to ¼", and remove all marking lines. Block and press the pillow front (see page 21).
7. Keeping the middle line of Chain Stitch centered, trim the pillow front to 15" square.
8. With right sides facing, stitch the front and back together, taking a ½" seam allowance and following the instructions on pages 48–49 for the type of backing you chose.
9. Make four tassels from the wool yarn, two of gold and two of chartreuse (see page 52). Using the pair of long tails at the top of the tassel as ties, attach one tassel at each of the four corners.
10. Stuff with pillow insert.

Dancing the Polka (Dot)

Simple designs are often the most successful. When I'm at a loss for an idea, I go back to basic childhood art forms, like stripes and polka dots. This trio of pillows interprets dots many ways — randomly placed polka dots in miniature and bolder versions, and large and overlapping circles. One simple idea fuels many variations. Each pillow is beautiful on its own, but together they make a *to the point* statement.

The yellow pillow is easiest to make, with its French Knots in worsted-weight wool knitting yarn randomly splashed over the linen surface. Corner pompoms give it a playful, childlike appeal. The melon-colored pillow is scattered with larger polka dots stitched in glossy mercerized cotton, creating an interesting textural contrast to the linen ground fabric. The blue-gray pillow features overlapping, larger dots filled in Chain Stitch with varied-color wool yarns for a contemporary graphic look.

Plastic pompom makers are inexpensive and let you quickly make four different sizes of dense, beautifully shaped pompoms. I like making pompoms the old-fashioned way, by wrapping wool yarn around a piece of cardboard. You'll need yarn (amount depends on size of pompom), a small piece of cardboard from a corrugated box, cellophane tape, and sharp scissors.

1. Cut two pieces of cardboard 3" x 4". Hold the pieces of cardboard together and wrap cellophane packing tape around them, fastening the pieces together and covering all the edges with tape. (This makes it easy to slide the yarn off in step 3.)

2. Cut a piece of sturdy yarn 10" long. Set this piece aside.

3. Tightly wrap the pompom yarn around the cardboard, layering it as shown. The more yarn you wrap, the thicker and denser the pompom will be: 120 wraps makes a nice thick pompom. Cut end of yarn and carefully slide the bundle of yarn off the cardboard.

Tip: You can speed this process by drawing yarn from two skeins of yarn at once.

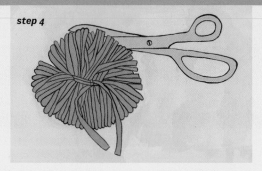

step 4

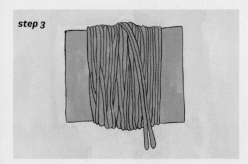

step 3

4. Wrap the 10" piece of yarn as tightly as you can around the bundle of yarns at the midpoint (like a cinched-in waistline), and tie a firm knot. Flip the pompom over and tie a second knot. Leave the ends long to attach the pompom to a project. Clip all the loops, and trim any uneven strands to shape the pompom into a fluffy ball.

MORE THOUGHTS ON POMPOMS

• Odds and ends of knitting and crochet yarn (your "stash") make great pompoms.

• Multi-colored pompoms are very festive! Wind two different colors together for a tweed, or for a really colorful pompom, use five complementary colors of yarn. As you wind the yarn, break it every so often to add a second, third, fourth, and fifth color.

• You can use all those trimmings to stuff small objects such as toys and pincushions. My young daughter loves to glue them on paper to create her own fluffy designs.

mini-dots

FINISHED SIZE: 16" x 16"

FABRICS

⅝ yard yellow suit-weight linen, for pillow front

⅝ yard checked cotton fabric, for pillow back (or use the same linen as the ground fabric)

THREAD

Any pink worsted-weight wool knitting yarn

I used Nashua Handknits Julia (50% wool/25% alpaca/ 25% mohair), 93 yd (85 m)/1.75 oz (50 gm) skeins: one skein in Zinnia Pink/5084.

NOTIONS

Size 18 chenille needle

Embroidery hoop

16" square pillow insert (preferably down)

STITCHES

French Knot (page 29)

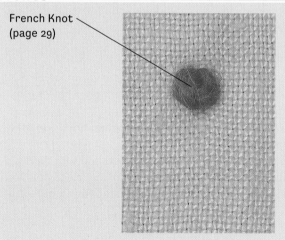

PREPARING THE PILLOW FRONT AND BACK

1. Measure and cut a 19" square from the linen for the pillow front (see page 44).
2. Measure and cut the pillow back fabric for either a non-removable cover or a flapped back opening for a 16" square pillow (see page 48). Set pillow back aside.

STITCHING THE DESIGN

3. Work French Knots randomly spaced over the entire surface of the fabric. Carry the yarn across the back of the fabric as you are working, but to avoid distorting the fabric, make sure you do not pull the yarn too tightly. If you use an embroidery hoop, you'll find it helps to keep the tension loose. (See To Hoop or Not to Hoop? page 45.)

FINISHING THE PILLOW

4. Neaten the thread ends by trimming to ¼", and remove all marking lines. Block and press the pillow front, (see page 21).
5. Trim the pillow front to 17" square, taking care to keep the design centered (see page 47).
6. With right sides facing, stitch the front and back together, taking a ½" seam allowance and following the instructions on pages 48–49 for the type of backing you chose.
7. Using the same yarn you used for the French Knots, make four pompoms (see page 58). Trim the pompoms to 1½". Attach one pompom at each corner of the pillow, as follows: Thread each of the two tying threads through a tapestry needle, one by one, and use the needle to draw each thread through to the back of the fabric about ⅛" apart. Knot the tying threads together, and trim.
8. Stuff with pillow insert.

satin dots

FINISHED SIZE: 12" x 18"

FABRICS

½ yard melon suit-weight linen, for pillow front

½ yard of silk, linen, or cotton fabric, for pillow back (or use the same linen as the ground fabric)

THREAD

Two size 5 skeins of brown pearl cotton

I used DMC 610 (brown).

NOTIONS

Size 20 chenille needle

Embroidery hoop

14 dimes, to use as circle templates

12" x 18" pillow insert (preferably down)

STITCHES

Satin Stitch (page 23)

Backstitch (page 24)

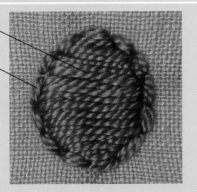

PREPARING THE PILLOW FRONT AND BACK

1. Measure and cut a 15" × 21" rectangle from the linen for the pillow front (see page 44).
2. Measure and cut the pillow back fabric for either a non-removable cover or a flapped back opening for a 12" × 18" pillow (see page 48). Set pillow back aside.
3. Working on a flat surface, arrange the coins in a pleasing manner on the fabric, leaving the 1½" extra seam allowance around all four sides uncovered. Using a water-soluble or child's washable marker or lead pencil, trace around the coins.

STITCHING THE DESIGN

4. Using a doubled thread, fill in all the circles with Satin Stitch. Take care to work your Satin Stitches so that the threads stay parallel to the vertical threads of the fabric. I find that using an embroidery hoop helps me avoid puckering the fabric. (See To Hoop or Not to Hoop?, page 45.)
5. Using a doubled thread, work Backstitch around all of the circles. This gives the circles a nice, neat edge.

FINISHING THE PILLOW

6. Neaten the thread ends by trimming to ¼", and remove all marking lines. Block and press the completed piece (see page 21).
7. Trim the pillow front to 13" × 19", taking care to keep the design centered.
8. With right sides facing, stitch the front and back together, taking a ½" seam allowance and following the instructions on pages 48–49) for the type of backing you chose.
9. Stuff with pillow insert.

overlapping dots

Don't worry if there is a little show-through on the fabric beneath the stitches. They needn't be perfect!

FINISHED SIZE: 14" x 14"

FABRICS

⅝ yard gray suit-weight linen, for pillow front

⅝ yard cotton or linen fabric, for pillow back (or use the same linen as the ground fabric)

THREAD

One 8-yard skein of 3-ply Persian wool *each* of brown, pink, and cream

I used Paternayan, Honey Gold/731, Dusty Pink/913, and Old Gold/754.

NOTIONS

Size 20 chenille needle

14" square pillow insert (preferably down)

STITCHES

Chain Stitch
(page 26)

PREPARING THE PILLOW FRONT AND BACK

1. Measure and cut a 17" square from the linen for the pillow front (see page 44).
2. Measure and cut the pillow back fabric for either a non-removable cover or a flapped back opening for a 14" square pillow (see page 48). Set pillow back aside.
3. Use a photocopier to enlarge the Overlapping Dots pattern on page 182 by 333%. Making sure the design is centered, use the light table method to transfer the design to the fabric (see page 19).

STITCHING THE DESIGN

Note: For color references, see the pattern on page 182.

4. Using a single strand of Persian wool, and beginning at outside of a full circle, work ¼" to ⁵⁄₁₆" Chain Stitches. Work in a spiral toward center, packing stitches closely together row by row. The circular stitching may distort the fabric, but blocking will smooth this. Complete the six full circles in the same manner.
5. Fill in the partial circles, simulating the spirals in the full circles. When you come to a completed full circle, simply turn and begin the adjacent row close to the one you just worked.

FINISHING THE PILLOW

6. Neaten the thread ends by trimming to ¼", and remove all marking lines. Block and press the completed piece (see page 21). When blocking this pillow, use lots of steam to flatten out the Chain Stitch areas.
7. Trim the pillow front to 15" square, taking care to keep the design centered (see page 47).
8. With right sides facing, stitch the front and back together, taking a ½" seam allowance and following the instructions on pages 48–49 for the type of backing you chose.
9. Stuff with pillow insert.

Naturally Inspired

As long as there's been embroidery, nature has been a popular stitchery theme, both elaborate and simple, in opulent as well as common threads. Many museums have examples of centuries-old stitcheries featuring nature in all forms — including plants, flowers, animals, birds, seashells, and even landscapes.

As an introduction to stitching naturally inspired designs, I've chosen three motifs: a Tuscan tree, undersea coral, and a simple vinelike line. Each is stitched in a single color, so you can concentrate on some new techniques without worrying about changing colors. Sample these projects to learn about the variety of effects you can produce with needle and thread.

Wool fabric and wool yarn make forgiving materials for first-time stitchers, although you could also choose linen or cotton fabrics for these designs. I ran the wool fabric for this pillow through a hot-water wash/cold rinse once to felt it lightly. (For information on felting, see page 46.)

FINISHED SIZE: 12" x 18"

FABRICS

½ yard light-turquoise wool, washed and slightly felted, for the pillow front

½ yard print cotton or linen fabric, for pillow back

THREAD

Three 8-yard skeins of 3-ply, teal blue Persian wool, or about 24 yards of any worsted-weight wool knitting yarn

I used Paternayan, Teal Blue/521.

NOTIONS

Size 18 chenille needle

12" x 18" pillow insert (preferably down)

STITCHES

Fishbone Stitch (page 28)

Backstitch (page 24)

Stem Stitch (page 25)

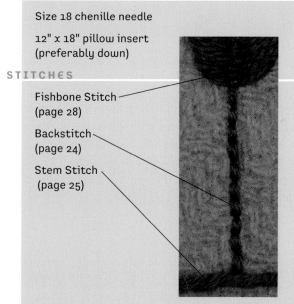

PREPARING THE PILLOW FRONT AND BACK

1. Measure and cut a 15" × 21" rectangle (see page 44).
2. Measure and cut the pillow back fabric for either a non-removable cover or a flapped back opening for a 12" × 18" pillow (see page 48). Set pillow back aside.
3. Use a photocopier to increase the Tuscan Trees pattern on page 182 by 200%. Making sure the design is centered, transfer the design to the fabric using the tracing paper method (see page 19). Darken the lines by re-drawing them with a water-soluble or child's washable marker.

STITCHING THE DESIGN

Note: Use all three plies of the Persian wool or one strand of knitting worsted wool to work all of the stitches in this design.

4. Work the horizontal ground line in Stem Stitch.
5. Work the trunks of each tree in Backstitch.
6. Work the top portion of each tree in Fishbone Stitch.

FINISHING THE PILLOW

7. Neaten the thread ends by trimming to ¼", and remove all marking lines. Block and press the completed piece (see page 21).
8. Trim the pillow front to 13" × 19", taking care to keep the design centered (see page 47).
9. With right sides facing, stitch the front and back together, taking a ½" seam allowance, and following the instructions on pages 48–49 for the type of backing you chose.
10. Stuff with pillow insert.

under-the-sea coral

FINISHED SIZE: 16" x 16"

FABRICS

⅝ yard light pink, medium-weight wool, for pillow front

½ yard linen or cotton fabric print, for pillow back

THREAD

One 8-yard skein of 3-ply, red-orange Persian wool, or about 24 yards of any worsted-weight wool knitting yarn

I used Paternayan, Spice/ 850.

NOTIONS

Size 20 chenille needle

16" square pillow insert (preferably down)

STITCHES

Stem Stitch (page 25)

Feather Stitch (page 28)

PREPARING THE PILLOW FRONT AND BACK

1. Measure and cut a 19" square from the wool for the pillow front (see page 44).
2. Measure and cut the pillow back fabric for either a non-removable cover or a flapped back opening for a 16" square pillow (see page 48). Set pillow back aside.
3. Use a photocopier to increase the Under-the-Sea Coral pattern on page 182 by 333%. Making sure the design is centered, transfer the design to the fabric using the tracing paper method (see page 19. Darken the lines by re-drawing them with a water-soluble or child's washable marker.

STITCHING THE DESIGN

Note: Use two plies of the Persian wool or one strand of knitting worsted wool to work all of the stitches in this design.

4. Work the wavy horizon line in Stem Stitch.
5. Work the branches of the coral in Feather Stitch. Complete all of the main sections, then stitch the side branches.
   Note: The pattern indicates only the center line of the Feather Stitch. Work the left and right parts of the feather in random lengths and angles for a natural, free-form look.

FINISHING THE PILLOW

6. Neaten the thread ends by trimming to ¼", and remove all marking lines. Block and press the pillow front (see page 21).
7. Trim the pillow front to 17" square, taking care to keep the design centered (see page 47).
8. With right sides facing, stitch the front and back together, taking a ½" seam allowance and following the instructions on pages 48–49 for the type of backing you chose.
9. Stuff with pillow insert.

loopy vine

FINISHED SIZE: 14" x 14"

FABRICS

½ yard citrus green, medium-weight wool, for pillow front

½ yard cotton or silk fabric, for pillow back

THREAD

One 8-yard skein of 3-ply, loden green Persian wool

I used Paternayan, Loden Green/692.

NOTIONS

Size 20 chenille needle

14" pillow insert (preferably down)

STITCHES

Backstitch (page 24)

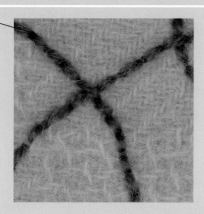

PREPARING THE PILLOW FRONT AND BACK

1. Measure and cut a 17" square from the wool for the pillow front (see page 44).
2. Measure and cut the pillow back fabric for either a non-removable cover or a flapped back opening for a 14" square pillow (see page 48). Set pillow back aside.
3. Use a photocopier to increase the Loopy Vine pattern on page 182 by 500%. Taking care to center the design, transfer the design to the fabric using the tracing paper method (page 19). Darken the lines by re-drawing them with a water-soluble or child's washable marker. Note: As an alternative to using the template, you can draw your own loopy lines freehand with a marker on the wool.

STITCHING THE DESIGN

4. Using one strand of Persian wool, work Backstitch over all the lines.

FINISHING THE PILLOW

5. Neaten the thread ends by trimming to ¼", and remove all marking lines. Block and press the pillow front (see page 21).
6. Trim the pillow front to 15" square, taking care to keep the design centered (see page 47).
7. With right sides facing, stitch the front and back together, taking a ½" seam allowance and following the instructions on pages 48–49 for the type of backing you chose.
8. Stuff with pillow insert.

Quirky Quotes

Do you have a special quote you would love to have live on *ad infinitum*? Stitched words not only become art, they inspire thought! Needlepointers often work hours and hours to stitch a quote on a pillow that adorns a couch. (Needlepoint is stitchery done on open-weave canvas.) I like the idea of using simple embroidery for the same purpose. The quote, depending on your choice, can inspire reflection, inspiration, or perhaps just a good laugh. The quotes on these two pillows are words I live by.

You might like to combine other motifs with your quote, as I did on the orange Creativity/Chaos pillow. I kept my pillows simple by working the stitchery in only one color, but you can expand on this classic idea by adding more motifs and colors for your own original design.

If you would like to stitch a different sentiment, choose a favorite quote of your own or pick one from this list. It's fun to collect ideas that you could use for future stitchery, so the next time you hear or read a good quotable, write it down. Here are some ideas to get you started:

Love conquers all.

Being bored is not allowed. ("Nanny," in Kay Thompson's *Eloise*)

There is always some madness in love. But there is also always some reason in madness. *(Friedrich Nietzsche)*

To fear love is to fear life, and those who fear life are already three parts dead. *(Bertrand Russell)*

Love is the triumph of imagination over intelligence. *(H. L. Mencken)*

Please give me some good advice in your next letter. I promise not to follow it. *(Edna St. Vincent Millay)*

The longer I live the more beautiful life becomes. *(Frank Lloyd Wright)*

I never feel age . . . If you have creative work, you don't have age or time. *(Louise Nevelson)*

A room without books is like a body without a soul. *(G. K. Chesterton)*

The secret to creativity is knowing how to hide your sources. *(Albert Einstein)*

To live a creative life, we must lose our fear of being wrong. *(Joseph Chilton Pearce)*

Every child is an artist. The problem is how to remain an artist once he grows up. *(Pablo Picasso)*

Things do not change; we change. *(Henry David Thoreau)*

Nothing endures but change. (Heraclitus)

A good home must be made, not bought. *(Joyce Maynard)*

To achieve great things we must live as though we were never going to die. *(Marquis de Vauvenargues)*

Everything you can imagine is real. *(Pablo Picasso)*

I am always doing that which I cannot do, in order that I may learn how to do it. *(Pablo Picasso)*

Once you've decided on your quote, type it out on your computer. Experiment with different typestyles and sizes to determine which one best suits the feeling of the quote. I chose a simple, contemporary-looking font called Avant Garde, because it's one of my favorites. Set your page up for landscape view, and enlarge the type as much as you can, so the words just fit the paper. Print, then increase the letters on a copy machine to the size you want for your pillow.

Your own handwriting can also be very expressive and quite beautiful for this project, although it may take a few tries before you get what you want. Write out your quote and then enlarge it on a photocopier until it is the desired size.

Striking Out on Your Own

Italian proverb

FINISHED SIZE: 12" x 18"

FABRICS

½ yard yellow suit-weight linen, for pillow front

½ yard striped cotton fabric, for pillow back (or use the same linen as the ground fabric)

THREAD

One 8-yard skein of 3-ply, rust Persian wool, or one 8.7-yard, 6-strand skein of rust cotton embroidery floss

I used Paternayan, Spice/850.

NOTIONS

Size 20 chenille needle

12" x 18" pillow insert (preferably down)

STITCHES

Backstitch
(page 24)

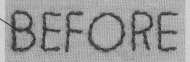

PREPARING THE PILLOW FRONT AND BACK

1. Measure and cut a 15" × 21" rectangle (see page 144).
2. Measure and cut the pillow back fabric for either a non-removable cover or a flapped back opening for a 12" × 18" pillow (see page 48). Set pillow back aside.
3. Type the quote on your computer in Avant Garde or other simple type font. Use as large a typeface as possible, print it out, then increase the type size on a photocopier to the desired size.
4. Transfer the words to your fabric using a light table or tracing paper (see page 19).

STITCHING THE DESIGN

5. Using a single strand of wool or three strands of cotton embroidery floss, work all the letters in Backstitch. To avoid *floats* (threads that you carry across the back of the work to the next point of entry) that may show through, tie off the thread at the end of each letter on the back of the fabric using a stitched knot (see page 20), and begin the next letter anew.

FINISHING THE PILLOW

6. Neaten the thread ends by trimming to ¼", and remove all marking lines. Block and press the pillow front (see page 21).
7. Trim the pillow front to 13" × 19", taking care to keep the design centered (see page 47).
8. With right sides facing, stitch the front and back together, taking a ½" seam allowance and following the instructions on pages 48–49 for the type of backing you choose.
9. Stuff with pillow insert.

creativity/chaos

FINISHED SIZE: 16" x 16"

FABRICS

⅝ yard orange suit-weight linen, for pillow front

⅝ yard cotton fabric, for pillow back (or use the same linen as the ground fabric)

THREAD

One 8-yard skein of 3-ply, dark brown Persian wool, or one 8.7-yard, 6-strand skein of cotton embroidery floss

I used Paternayan, Coffee Brown/420.

NOTIONS

Size 20 chenille needle

16" pillow insert
(preferably down)

STITCHES

Backstitch
(page 24)

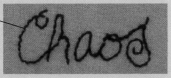

PREPARING THE PILLOW FRONT AND BACK

1. Measure and cut a 19" square from the linen for the pillow front (see page 44).
2. Measure and cut the pillow back fabric for either a non-removable cover or a flapped back opening for a 16" square pillow (see page 48). Set pillow back aside.
3. Use a photocopier to increase the Creativity/Chaos pattern on page 183 by 286%. Making sure the design is centered, transfer the quote and swirled-heart design to the linen fabric using either a light table or tracing paper (see page 19).

STITCHING THE DESIGN

4. Using a single strand of wool, work both the quote and the heart motifs in Backstitch.

FINISHING THE PILLOW

5. Neaten the thread ends by trimming to ¼", and remove all marking lines. Block and press the pillow front (see page 21).
6. Trim the pillow front to 17" square, taking care to keep the design centered (see page 47). Finish as for preceding project.

get personal!

Monograms are hot once again! This little 12"-square wool pillow uses the classic format of two smaller initials surrounding the large final initial. The lettering is worked with one strand of Persian wool in closely packed Stem Stitch and the border in Running Stitch. The large letter is 2½" tall, the smaller letters are 1¼" tall, and the diamond is 7½" tall and wide.

Sample This!

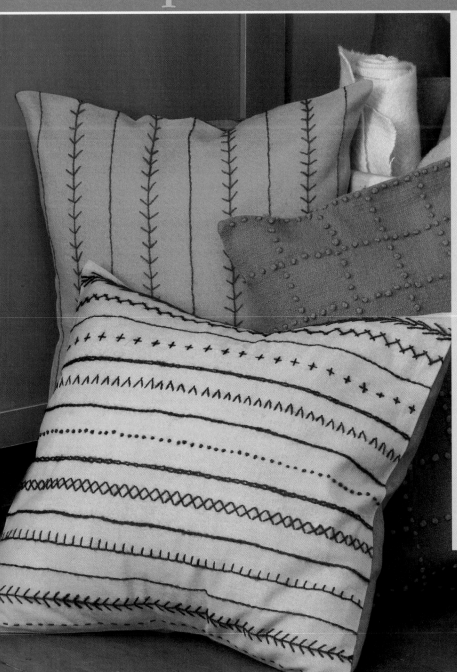

I like this pillow collection because the pillows look modern in every sense of the word, but in fact they are as old fashioned as a classic sampler from the 1700s. To give your pillows an off-beat, one-of-a-kind look, choose funky color combinations of ground fabric and thread, such as chartreuse and fuchsia or brown and turquoise.

Once a row of stitches on any one of these samplers is complete, if your quest for perfection gets to you and you're not satisfied with the beginning of the row, you can easily rip out the first few stitches and re-stitch them to make them as good as the rest. On the other hand, I think it's better to leave them just the way they are, as a reminder of what it was like to learn to stitch.

The pumpkin-colored pillow is a perfect first project, because it features a sampling of twelve different embroidery stitches worked in stripes, one stripe for each stitch. By the time you've practiced a stitch all the way across a row, you will have perfected that stitching technique.

sampler stripes

It's important to maintain an even stitch height for some stitches on this sampler.

Tip: Build stitches evenly on each side of the guideline by keeping it centered. You may want to draw ¼" lines on each side of it until you've had more practice at keeping stitches consistent.

FINISHED SIZE: 16" x 16"

FABRICS

⅝ yard quilting cotton or suit-weight linen, for pillow front

½ yard fabric, for pillow back (or use the same cotton as the ground fabric)

THREAD

One 8-yard skein of 3-ply, dark brown Persian wool

I used Paternayan, Coffee Brown/420.

NOTIONS

Size 20 chenille needle

16" square pillow insert (preferably down)

STITCHES

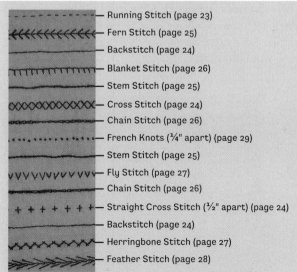

— Running Stitch (page 23)
— Fern Stitch (page 25)
— Backstitch (page 24)
— Blanket Stitch (page 26)
— Stem Stitch (page 25)
— Cross Stitch (page 24)
— Chain Stitch (page 26)
— French Knots (¼" apart) (page 29)
— Stem Stitch (page 25)
— Fly Stitch (page 27)
— Chain Stitch (page 26)
— Straight Cross Stitch (½" apart) (page 24)
— Backstitch (page 24)
— Herringbone Stitch (page 27)
— Feather Stitch (page 28)

PREPARING THE PILLOW FRONT AND BACK

1. Measure and cut a 19" square for pillow front (see page 44).
2. Measure and cut the pillow back fabric for either a non-removable cover or a flapped back opening for a 16" square pillow (see page 48). Set pillow back aside.
3. Using a see-through ruler and a water-soluble or child's washable marker and beginning 2½" in from one edge, draw 15 lines, spaced 1" apart across the fabric (see diagram, page 186).

STITCHING THE DESIGN

4. Beginning 1" in from the edge, work one kind of stitch along the first line, ending 1" in from the opposite edge. Work a different stitch along each of the 15 guidelines. My order of stitching is shown at the left, but you should feel free to make up your own design.

FINISHING THE PILLOW

5. Neaten the thread ends by trimming to ¼", and remove all marking lines. Block and press the pillow front (see page 21).
6. Trim the pillow front to 17" square, taking care to keep the design centered (see page 47).
7. With right sides facing, stitch the front and back together, taking a ½" seam allowance and following the instructions on pages 48–49 for the type of backing you chose.
8. Stuff with pillow insert.

fern & backstitch on pink

The stripes on this pink pillow feature only two alternating stitches: Backstitch and Fern Stitch. If you can't keep the width of Fern Stitch consistent, draw guidelines ¼" away from the stitching line on each side. I prefer that every stitch isn't perfect, and so I "guesstimate" the width of each stitch as I go. After all, perfection isn't all it's cracked up to be!

FINISHED SIZE: 14" x 14"

FABRICS

½ yard suit-weight linen, for pillow front

½ yard linen or cotton fabric, for pillow back (or use the same linen as the ground fabric)

THREAD

One 8-yard skein of 3-ply, rust Persian wool.

I used Paternayan, Spice/850.

NOTIONS

Size 20 chenille needle

14" square pillow insert (preferably down)

STITCHES

Backstitch (page 24)

Fern Stitch (page 25)

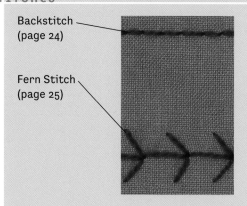

PREPARING THE PILLOW FRONT AND BACK

1. Measure and cut a 17" square from the linen for the pillow front (see page 44).
2. Measure and cut the pillow back fabric for either a non-removable cover or a flapped back opening for a 14" square pillow (see page 48). Set pillow back aside.
3. Using a see-through ruler and a water-soluble or child's washable marker or lead pencil and starting 2½" from one edge, draw nine lines, spaced 1½" apart (see diagram, page 187).

STITCHING THE DESIGN

4. Beginning 1" in from the edge of the fabric, work the first (simple) stripe in Backstitch to within 1" of the opposite edge.
5. For the second (jagged) stripe, work the next line in Fern Stitch, again beginning and ending 1" in from the edge.
6. Continue alternating lines of Backstitch and Fern Stitch until all nine stripes are complete.

FINISHING THE PILLOW

7. Neaten the thread ends by trimming to ¼", and remove all marking lines. Block and press pillow front (see page 21).
8. Trim pillow front to 15" square, keeping the design centered.
9. With right sides facing, stitch the front and back together, taking a ½" seam allowance and following the instructions on pages 48–49 for the type of backing you chose.
10. Stuff with pillow insert.

French knot plaid

The idea for this pillow comes from an old-fashioned embroidery technique called candlewicking. Colonial Americans used the cotton string made for candle wicks to work elaborate patterns in French Knots on cotton fabric to create a very textured, bobble-like effect. I simplified the traditional format by designing a "plaid." I like the especially large, lumpy French Knot I can get with knitting yarn.

FINISHED SIZE: 12" x 18"

FABRICS

½ yard teal 100% wool fabric, machine-washed to slightly felt it, for pillow front

½ yard of cotton or linen fabric, for pillow back

THREAD

One skein of any smooth, worsted-weight pink wool knitting yarn

I used Nashua Handknits Julia (50% wool/25% alpaca/25% mohair), 93 yd (85 m)/1.75 oz (50 gm) skeins in Zinnia Pink/5084.

NOTIONS

Size 14 chenille needle

12" x 18" pillow insert (preferably down)

STITCHES

French Knots
(page 29)

PREPARING THE PILLOW FRONT AND BACK

1. Measure and cut a rectangular piece of fabric 15" × 21" (see page 44).
2. Measure and cut the pillow back fabric for either a non-removable cover or a flapped back opening for a 12" × 18" pillow (see page 48). Set pillow back aside.
3. Referring to the diagram on page 187, use a see-through ruler and a water-soluble or child's washable marker to draw five horizontal lines, spaced 2" apart, with the middle line centered on the fabric, and nine vertical lines, also spaced 2" apart and centered on the fabric, to make a regular grid. Begin the horizontal lines 3½" from the edge; begin the vertical lines 2½" in from the edge.

STITCHING THE DESIGN

4. Beginning 1" in from the edge, and spacing stitches about ⅜" away from each other, make a series of French Knots along one of the guidelines. Spacing needn't be exact. You're going for effect, not perfection. I try to place the same number of knots between each plaid crossing for a somewhat even look.
5. Continue working rows of French Knots along the guidelines until all vertical and horizontal lines are covered.

FINISHING THE PILLOW

6. Neaten the thread ends by trimming to ¼", and remove all marking lines. Block and press the pillow front (see page 21).
7. Trim the pillow front to 13" × 19", taking care to keep the design centered (see page 47).
8. With right sides facing, stitch the front and back together, taking a ½" seam allowance and following the instructions on page 48–49) for the type of backing you chose.
9. Stuff with pillow insert.

In a box of fabrics at the Brimfield (Massachusetts) Flea Market, I stumbled upon a nice, old, checked apron on which someone had embroidered a series of colored Xs in a line of white checks on the gingham. I was immediately enamored by the quaint look, dug deeper into the box, and was delighted to find more embroidered aprons, each with hand-stitched designs. Some were simply executed in striped or diamond patterns, while others featured intricately shaped flowers and butterflies. Those aprons inspired these pillows, which are made of heavy cotton gingham from an interior-decorating store.

green-and-white gingham

In my updated version of the gingham aprons, I chose to stitch the Xs in a diamond pattern, but you can develop your own ideas.

FINISHED SIZE: 16" x 16"

FABRICS

⅝ yard green-and-white gingham check (with ½" checks), for pillow front

⅝ yard cotton or silk print fabric, for pillow back

THREAD

One 8.7-yard, 6-strand skein of coral cotton embroidery floss

I used DMC 3832 (coral).

NOTIONS

Size 18 chenille needle

16" square pillow insert
(preferably down)

STITCHES

Cross Stitch
(page 24)

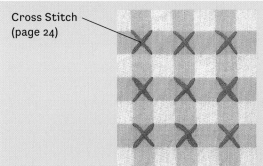

PREPARING THE PILLOW FRONT AND BACK

1. Measure and cut a 19" square from gingham for pillow front. Use the checks as a cutting guide, keeping either all-white or all-green checks around edge. This may result in a slightly different-sized pillow, but that will not matter.
2. Measure and cut the pillow back fabric for either a non-removable cover or a flapped back opening for a 16" square pillow. (See page 48.) Set pillow back aside.
3. Find the center point of the pillow front (see page 18), and adjust so that it falls on an all-green check. Use a water-soluble or child's washable marker to mark the center point. You will build the entire diamond around this center point.
4. Use your marker to draw the diamond-shaped guideline for your design, as follows: Count over five all-green checks on each side of the center check, both horizontally and vertically, and mark each of these checks with an X (eleven Xs both vertically and horizontally). Connect the outer Xs on all four sides. (See diagram on page 187.)

STITCHING THE DESIGN

5. Using six strands of floss, work one Cross Stitch on each all-green check within the diamond you marked in step 4. Begin by working the first half of Cross Stitch in one direction over entire pattern. Take care to use the outside edge of each check as your guide, so that all the checks will be the same size.
6. Work the second half of the Xs in the opposite direction.

FINISHING THE PILLOW

7. Neaten thread ends by trimming to ¼", and remove all marking lines. Block and press pillow front (see page 21.
8. Trim the pillow front to 17" square, taking care to keep the design centered (see page 47).
9. With right sides facing, stitch the front and back together, taking a ½" seam and following the instructions on pages 48–49 for the type of backing you chose.
10. Stuff with pillow insert.

blue-and-white gingham

You can use any sized check for this technique, although the floats may become too long on a super-sized check. It's fun to see how totally different the completed project looks, depending on whether you make your tiny Xs on white or colored checks.

FINISHED SIZE: 16" x 16"

FABRICS

⅝ yard blue-and-white gingham check (with ½" checks), for pillow front

⅝ yard cotton or silk print fabric, for pillow back

THREAD

One 8.7-yard, 6-strand skein of green cotton embroidery floss

I used Anchor 256 (green).

NOTIONS

Size 18 chenille needle

16" square pillow insert (preferably down)

STITCHES

Cross Stitch (page 24)

PREPARING THE PILLOW FRONT AND BACK

1. Follow steps 1–4 for the Green-and-White Gingham pillow, but for this pillow, mark all-white checks, instead of all-green ones.

STITCHING THE DESIGN

2. Using all six strands of cotton floss, work one Cross Stitch on each all-white check within the diamond. Continue as for the Green-and-White Gingham pillow, steps 5 and 6.

FINISHING THE PILLOW

Complete pillow as for Green-and-White Gingham pillow.

salmon-and-white gingham

This pillow features smaller ¼" checks, but the technique is the same as for the other versions.

FINISHED SIZE: 16" x 16"

FABRICS

⅝ yard salmon-and-white gingham check (with ¼" checks), for pillow front

⅝ yard cotton or silk print fabric, for pillow back

THREAD

Two 8.7-yard, 6-strand skeins of blue cotton embroidery floss

I used DMC 792 (blue).

NOTIONS

Size 18 chenille needle

16" square pillow insert (preferably down)

STITCHES

Cross Stitch (page 24)

PREPARING THE PILLOW FRONT AND BACK

1. Follow steps 1–4 for the Green-and-White Gingham pillow, but because this fabric features smaller checks, mark 17 Xs both vertically and horizontally.

STITCHING THE DESIGN

2. Using all six strands of cotton floss, work one Cross Stitch on each all-white check within the diamond. Continue as for the Green-and-White Gingham pillow, steps 5 and 6.

FINISHING THE PILLOW

Complete pillow as for Green-and-White Gingham pillow.

Decorating gingham cloth aprons with Cross Stitch was very popular in the 1940s and '50s — the days when women wore aprons! Every kitchen had a drawer full of a variety of styles, from aprons for casual cooking to those for fancy cocktail parties. And now, aprons are back, and they are also becoming collectibles in the antique market!

Aprons were usually one of the first sewing projects in home economics — the class every girl *had* to take in seventh and eighth grade, the class in which she learned the basics of sewing and cooking. Gingham was ideal for beginners because the checks served as easy-to-follow guidelines for stitchery and seams. The project combined learning some hand-sewing techniques (the Cross Stitches) with the mastering of the sewing machine.

Popular with women of all ages, Cross Stitch patterns for these gingham aprons were available in sewing shops and through mail-order sources. Geometrics, florals, quiltlike star motifs, vines, teapots — the design possibilities were seemingly endless. Some girls added rickrack, or they combined Cross Stitch with Straight Cross Stitch or created Needlewoven leaves.

To learn more about gingham aprons, see Judy Florence's *Gingham Aprons of the '40s and '50s* (Schiffer Publishing, 2003).

Cross Stitch on Windowpane

For these pillows, I used the intersections on a unique, open plaid known as windowpane as a backdrop for some easy stitches, such as Straight Stitch, Cross Stitch, and Lazy Daisy Stitch. It may look complicated, but once you try it, you'll realize how simple it really is.

FINISHED SIZE: 14" x 14"

FABRICS

½ yard blue-and-white windowpane plaid fabric, for pillow front

½ yard cotton check fabric, for pillow back

THREAD

One 8.7-yard, 6-strand skein *each* of fuchsia and green cotton embroidery floss

I used DMC 3607 (fuchsia) and 906 (green).

NOTIONS

Size 20 chenille needle

14" square pillow insert (preferably down)

STITCHES

Cross Stitch
(page 24)

Straight Cross Stitch
(page 24)

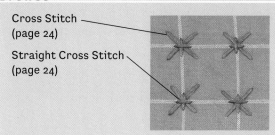

PREPARING THE PILLOW FRONT AND BACK

1. With a see-through ruler, measure and cut a 17" square, using the lines of the plaid as a guide. (You can draw your line along a plaid line or evenly spaced away from one.) It's okay if the square ends up a little bigger or smaller than 17".

2. Measure and cut the pillow back fabric for either a non-removable cover or a flapped back opening for a 14" square pillow. (See page 44.) Set pillow back aside.

3. Referring to the diagram on page 188, use a see-through ruler and a water-soluble pen to draw a pair of ½"-wide guidelines centered over the white stripe that is about 2½" in from an edge; repeat on the next white stripe in. Do this on all four sides of the fabric.

STITCHING THE DESIGN

4. Using all six strands of the green cotton embroidery floss (as it comes from the skein), work one Cross Stitch where each white plaid line intersects the guidelines you drew in step 3. Try to make the Xs as square as possible; they should measure about ½" square. Cover all the intersecting white plaid lines within the guidelines with Cross Stitch.

5. Using six strands of the fuchsia cotton embroidery floss, work one Upright Cross Stitch on top of each green X. The fuchsia stitches should be about ¼" long.

FINISHING THE PILLOW

6. Neaten the thread ends by trimming to ¼", and remove all marking lines. Block and press the pillow front, (see page 21). Remove any water-soluble marks.

7. Trim the pillow front to 15" square, taking care to keep the design centered (see page 47).

8. With right sides facing, stitch the front and back together, taking a ½" seam and following the instructions on pages 48–49 for the type of backing you chose.

9. Stuff with pillow insert.

green-and-white windowpane plaid

For this variation on the blue-and-white pillow, instead of a stitched border, I worked a square in the center of the pillow using a simple Straight Stitch.

FINISHED SIZE: 16" x 16"

FABRICS

⅝ yard green-and-white windowpane plaid fabric, for pillow front

⅝ yard cotton check fabric, for pillow back

THREAD

One 8.7-yard, 6-strand skein of fuchsia cotton embroidery floss

I used Anchor 77 (fuchsia).

NOTIONS

Size 20 chenille needle

16" square pillow insert (preferably down)

STITCHES

Straight Stitch (page 24)

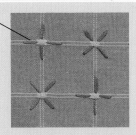

PREPARING THE PILLOW FRONT AND BACK

1. Use a see-through ruler to measure a 19" square, using the plaid lines as a guide. (In order to follow the plaid lines, you may have to make the square a little bigger or smaller than 19", but that's okay. It doesn't hurt to fudge a bit, if you get it as close as you can.) Cut along the lines.

2. Measure and cut the pillow back fabric for either a non-removable cover or a flapped back opening for a 16" square pillow (see page 48). Set pillow back aside.

3. Fold the fabric to find the center plaid line in both directions. Referring to the diagram on page 188, use a water-soluble or child's washable marker to mark the intersecting lines nearest the center with a large cross (+) for the center point. Count out three plaid lines in each direction from this point. The outermost crosses mark the height and width of the stitching area. Draw guidelines through these points horizontally and vertically to frame the area. You will place decorative stitching at each intersection of plaid lines within this box.

STITCHING THE DESIGN

4. Using six strands of the fuchsia embroidery floss, work Straight Stitch at each intersection within the area marked in step 3. Note that Xs and crosses are alternated throughout the design.

FINISHING THE PILLOW

5. Neaten the thread ends by trimming to ¼", and remove all marking lines. Block and press the pillow front, (see page 21).

6. Trim the pillow front to 17" square, taking care to keep the design centered (see page 47).

7. With right sides facing, stitch the front and back together, taking a ½" seam and following the instructions on pages 48–49 for the type of backing you choose. Use the plaid lines as a stitching guide.

8. Stuff with pillow insert.

pink-and-white dishtowel pillow

Made from a dishtowel, this plaid features large blocks of 16 smaller squares, with each large block defined by a group of thick and thin lines. In the middle of each large block, I placed a four-petaled Lazy Daisy flower, spiced up with an olive-colored French Knot center. Where the thick and thin plaid lines intersect, I placed small Cross Stitches in the same olive green to tie the design together. You're unlikely to find the same plaid, but you can use this idea as a starting point for your own design.

FINISHED SIZE: 16" x 16"

FABRICS

⅝ yard pink-and-white windowpane check fabric or dishtowel, for pillow front

⅝ yard contrasting cotton fabric, for pillow back

THREAD

One 8.7-yard, 6-strand skein of green and two skeins of fuchsia cotton embroidery floss

I used DMC 581 (fuchsia) and Anchor 77 (green).

NOTIONS

Size 20 chenille needle

16" square pillow insert (preferably down)

STITCHES

Lazy Daisy (page 27)

French Knot (page 29)

Cross Stitch (page 24)

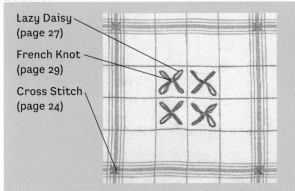

PREPARING THE PILLOW FRONT AND BACK

1. To prepare the pillow front, find the center point of the large central block and mark it with a water-soluble or child's washable marker. Draw a square about 19" around this center point, using the plaid lines as your guide. Cut out the pillow front.

2. Measure and cut the pillow back fabric for either a non-removable cover or a flapped back opening for a 16" square pillow. (See page 48.) Set pillow back aside.

STITCHING THE DESIGN

3. Using all six strands of the fuchsia embroidery floss, make a lazy daisy with four "petals" (each petal is created with a separate Lazy Daisy Stitch) in the center four boxes within each of the large blocks. The flower will resemble an X.

4. Using the olive green floss, stitch a French Knot in the center of each lazy daisy.

5. Using the olive green floss, make one Cross Stitch at the intersection of each group of thick and thin lines (at the corners of the large blocks).

FINISHING THE PILLOW

6. Neaten the thread ends by trimming to ¼", and remove all marking lines. Block and press the pillow front, (see page 21).

7. Trim the pillow front to 17" square, taking care to keep the design centered (see page 47).

8. With right sides facing, stitch the front and back together, taking a ½" seam, and following the instructions on pages 48–49 for the type of backing you chose. Use the plaid lines as a stitching guide.

9. Stuff with pillow insert.

Striped Dishtowel Pillows

Stripes come in all widths and colors, woven in two or more shades. They can be classic, traditional, and somber, or they can be bold and joyful. You'll find striped fabrics everywhere — in dressmaking fabrics, for home decorating, or even in colorful dishtowels, like these that I found in the kitchen department of my local food co-op. Dishtowels are usually made of pure cotton fibers or linen blends that make them soft and absorbent. Often they are cheerfully colored to brighten the task at hand. This makes them a great choice for sunny pillows reminiscent of a summer beach house.

I decorated my striped fabric with a mix of colors and stitches for a festive, Mexican-style look. After decorating the dishtowels, I sewed them into rectangular pillows that would look equally nice in a child's bedroom or on a porch. Or just use the stitched piece as a dishtowel!

Perhaps you've seen a framed piece of needlework in a museum or an antique store. The sampler tradition began in Europe, where the earliest known example dates from 1502. Made in England, France, Holland, Spain, and Italy, these designs were worked to make a decorative stripe or block on a narrow width of fabric. Pattern after pattern was added until a long piece of fabric was covered with different stripes. These samplers became the stitcher's pattern book, an important resource, since most households were not rich enough to own books.

When the Europeans colonized America, they brought their sampler-making skills with them, but they put a new spin on the old European tradition. Young American girls and women made samplers that resembled pictures that documented their family's history and used them to decorate their walls. At the time, most families had extremely modest homes with little decoration, so a sampler was often the only piece hanging on a wall. Remember, this was before the days of photography!

Stitching was an important part of every-day family life in Colonial America. There were no stores to shop for clothing, so each family made its own, often spinning and weaving the fabric as well. At school, young girls learned to stitch samplers on fabric at about the same time they learned to read and write. These learning samplers were most often worked in Cross Stitch and featured the alphabet and numbers and the girl's name.

Wealthier Colonial families sent their daughters to private schools, where they learned more sophisticated methods of stitching. They often created samplers depicting their homes and families, along with their name, birth date, the year the sampler was stitched, and sometimes a verse from the Bible or a favorite phrase. These samplers, made between the years of 1650 and 1850 are highly sought after by museums and textile collectors, with their price sometimes going into the tens of thousands of dollars.

To learn more about antique samplers, go to Carol and Stephen Huber's website: www.antiquesamplers.com, where you'll also find some incredible examples.

A Bit of History

festive blue stripes

When choosing colors to embellish the fabric, opt for shades that contrast greatly with the background stripe to guarantee that your handwork shows up against the fabric. For instance, on the light green stripes, I stitched with hot pink; for the dark red stripes, I chose a lighter shade of orange.

FINISHED SIZE: 16" x 21"

FABRICS

One striped dishtowel, or ⅞ yard of striped multi-color fabric, for pillow front

½ yard cotton fabric, for pillow back

THREAD

One 8.7-yard, 6-strand skein *each* of orange, pink, and cobalt blue cotton embroidery floss

I used Anchor 324 (orange), 57 (pink), and 134 (cobalt blue).

NOTIONS

Size 20 chenille needle

Polyester or cotton fill for stuffing (a pillow insert isn't available for this odd size)

STITCHES

Herringbone Stitch (page 27)

Feather Stitch (page 28)

Running Stitch (page 23)

Cross Stitch (page 24)

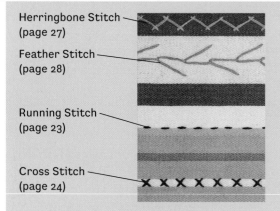

PREPARING THE PILLOW FRONT AND BACK

1. Cut a rectangle 19" × 24", with stripes running parallel to long edge. (A purchased dishtowel may be the correct size as is.)
2. Measure and cut the pillow back fabric for either a non-removable cover or a flapped back opening for a 16" × 21" pillow (see page 48). Set pillow back aside.
3. Analyze the stripes and experiment with different stitches in a small area. Rip your stitches out if you aren't happy with the color or the stitch. Once you have a general idea of what colors and stitches you want to use, proceed to step 4.

STITCHING THE DESIGN

4. Use three strands of cotton embroidery floss for these stitches. Don't begin your first stripe too close to the sewn edge, as it will be enclosed in the seam when you finish the pillow. The choice of colors and stitches is up to you, but for my design, I used the following patterns:

   - Herringbone Stitch in orange floss down the center of a red stripe
   - Feather Stitch in hot pink floss on the light green stripe
   - Running Stitch in cobalt blue floss to separate the narrow yellow and light orange stripes
   - Cross Stitch in cobalt blue on the small white stripe

FINISHING THE PILLOW

5. Neaten the thread ends by trimming to ¼", and remove all marking lines. Block and press the pillow front (see page 21). Remove any water-soluble marks.
6. *If you are using purchased fabric,* trim the pillow front to 17" × 22", taking care to keep the design centered (see page 47). *If you are using a dishtowel,* trim off the sewn hem to make the seams easier to stitch.
7. With right sides facing, stitch the front and back together, taking a ½" seam and following the instructions on pages 48–49 for the type of backing you chose.
8. Stuff with polyester or cotton fill.

sunny yellow stripes

Working on stripes is very rhythmic and soothing. I didn't mark my fabric with guidelines, but if you don't feel comfortable "eyeballing it" (see box at right), use a water-soluble or child's washable marker to rough out your design.

FINISHED SIZE: 16" x 21"

FABRICS

One striped dishtowel, or ⅞ yard of striped multi-color fabric, for pillow front

½ yard cotton fabric, for pillow back

THREAD

One 8.7-yard, 6-strand skein *each* of light yellow, rusty orange, and olive green; and two skeins of dark red embroidery floss

I used Anchor 288 (yellow), 326 (orange), 256 (green), and 1025 (red).

NOTIONS

Size 20 chenille needle

Polyester or cotton fill for stuffing (a pillow insert isn't available for this odd size)

STITCHES

Running Stitch (page 23)

Lazy Daisy (page 27)

French Knot (page 29)

Fern Stitch (page 25)

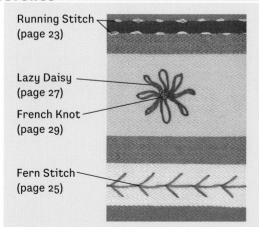

STITCHING DESIGN AND FINISHING PILLOW

Work and finish this pillow using the same guidelines listed for the Festive Blue Stripes pillow (page 84). My stitch pattern is as follows:

- Running Stitch in light yellow floss along each side of the small red stripe
- Fern Stitch in rusty orange floss along the center of the medium-sized white stripe
- Eight-petaled lazy daisies in dark red floss, spaced about 3" apart along wide stripe (seven flowers on each stripe)
- French Knots in olive green floss in center of each lazy daisy

eyeballing it

My mom always called guessing a measurement "eyeballing it," because you use your eyes and brain to judge the spacing of the stitches. They don't need to be perfect! You can also count on some standard measurements that you almost always have at hand. Here are my favorites:

In the U.S., a standard piece of paper is 8½" x 11". (Fold it in half for incremental measurements.)

A dollar bill is 6⅛" x 2⅝". Fold in half for a few more measurements. A penny measures ¾". Measurements of other coins are useful too.

My three middle fingernails measure ½" from cuticle to where the nail begins to grow. My pinky measures ⅜" around, and my thumb, ⅝". My thumb is 2¼" long. What do your fingers and nails measure?

This book measures 9" x 8¾". And the book itself makes a great ruler!

Get in the Groove

Corduroy makes its appearance

in fashion every few years, but in interior design it's always a standard. The word *corduroy* has a French flair, sounding much like the phrase *corde du roi*, which literally translates to "the king's cord." It's a woven fabric, created through a complex method of looping and cutting threads to make the distinctive textural ridges, or *wales*, which come in a wide variety of widths. I chose fabric with wales that are ¼" apart and used the wales as stitching lines for oversized Backstitch. It may look difficult, but it's actually super easy. Just count the wales and place the stitching evenly between every third wale — in other words, "stitch in the ditch." Don't choose a corduroy with a plasticized backing; it's too hard to get the needle through it. This design is time-consuming, but quite mindless, so it's a project you can work on when you can't — or don't want to — concentrate!

chartreuse pillow

FINISHED SIZE: 16" x 16"

FABRICS

⅝ yard chartreuse, wide-wale corduroy fabric, for pillow front

⅝ yard cotton or silk print fabric, for pillow back

THREAD

Two 8-yard, 3-ply skeins *each* of pink and red Persian wool

I used Paternayan, Hot Pink/962 and Spice/850.

NOTIONS

Size 20 chenille needle

16" square pillow insert (preferably down)

STITCHES

Backstitch
(page 24)

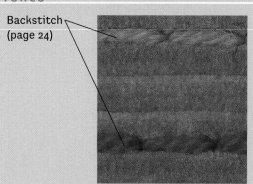

PREPARING THE PILLOW FRONT AND BACK

1. Measure and cut a 19" square of the corduroy for the pillow front (see page 44).
2. Measure and cut the pillow back fabric for either a non-removable cover or a flapped back opening for a 16" square pillow (see page 48). Set pillow back aside.

STITCHING THE DESIGN

3. Count seven wales (ridges) in from one of the edges. Using two plies of wool, work Backstitch in the "ditch" between this wale and the next. Make your stitches about ½" in length. Stitch the entire length of the fabric.
4. Count over three wales, and Backstitch in the next ditch with the second color.
5. Continue alternating yarn colors and stitching in each third ditch until the fabric is filled.

FINISHING THE PILLOW

6. Neaten the thread ends by trimming to ¼", and remove all marking lines. Block and press the pillow front, as shown on page 21.
7. Trim the pillow front to 17" square, taking care to keep the design centered (see page 47).
8. With right sides facing, stitch the front and back together, taking a ½" seam and following the instructions on pages 48–49 for the type of backing you chose.
9. Stuff with pillow insert.

red pillow

FINISHED SIZE: 16" x 16"

FABRICS

⅝ yard brick red, wide-wale corduroy fabric, for pillow front

½ yard linen or cotton print fabric, for pillow back

THREAD

Two 8-yard, 3-ply skeins *each* of pink, turquoise, and light green Persian wool

I used Paternayan, Hot Pink/962, Caribbean Blue/592, and Loden Green/694.

NOTIONS

Size 20 chenille needle

16" square pillow insert (preferably down)

STITCHES

Backstitch (page 24)

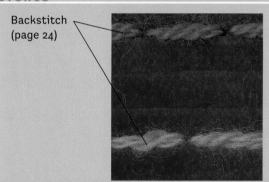

STITCHING THE DESIGN AND FINISHING THE PILLOW

Work and finish this pillow using the same guidelines written for the Chartreuse Pillow (page 88), except alternate the three colors every third ditch as follows: light green, pink, turquoise, and pink. Repeat this sequence until the fabric is filled.

the hunt is half the fun

When you're looking for pillow fabric, visit your fabric store with new eyes. Check your closet, the thrift shop, the local discount department store. Look at the stripes, plaids, checks, velvets, and corduroys. As you look, think about how you can use stitchery to enhance the fabric design. Be creative, and let yourself think outside the box.

You'll probably have a hard time finding exactly the same fabric I used for the pillows in this chapter. Don't think of this as a bad thing or let it stop you. When looking for fabrics, think about what stitches you can use to decorate the textiles you find — what colors and textures will bring excitement and a third dimension to the inherent beauty of the fabric. When you're done, you'll have an absolutely one-of-a-kind pillow that can't be duplicated. Have fun, and explore!

Playing with Plaids

i like to work embroidery on patterned fabrics, like plaids, checks, and stripes. By choosing contrasting colors for the stitching, I end up with a fabric that is quite out of the ordinary. I find that it takes a bit of skill to decide upon what colors to use, and many times, I start with what I think is a stellar color choice, only to end up ripping it out. I've learned to be patient. As your experience working with colors and patterns increases, you'll become more confident.

quilted diagonals

The highly textured surface of this quilted silk fabric features decorative, diamond-shaped machine stitching done at the factory. I used these ready-made diamonds as guides and frames for a simple pattern of Straight Stitches. The look is fancy embroidery, but the project couldn't be easier. If you can't find fabric similar to this, look for one with a woven or printed diamond pattern and embellish it in the same way.

FINISHED SIZE: 14" x 14"

FABRICS

½ yard dark brown, diamond-quilted silk fabric, for pillow front

½ yard silk fabric, for backing

THREAD

Four 8.7-yard, 6-strand skeins: two skeins of orange cotton embroidery floss and two skeins of gold

I used Anchor 326 (orange) and 907 (gold).

NOTIONS

Size 20 chenille needle

14" square pillow insert (preferably down)

STITCHES

Straight Stitch
(page 22)

Cross Stitch
(page 24)

Straight Cross Stitch
(page 24)

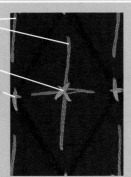

PREPARING THE PILLOW FRONT AND BACK

1. Measure and cut a 17" square from the quilted silk for the pillow front (see page 44).
2. Measure and cut the pillow back fabric for either a non-removable cover or a flapped back opening for a 14" square pillow (see page 48). Set pillow back aside.

STITCHING THE DESIGN

3. Using three strands of orange cotton floss, work a cross in Straight Stitch in one of the diamonds, beginning each arm of the cross at the center of the diamond. Fill each diamond in the same manner.
4. Using three strands of gold cotton floss, work one Cross Stitch over the center of each orange cross and one Straight Cross Stitch at each intersection of the machine-stitched lines. To avoid puckers, be sure to carry the thread loosely on the wrong side of the fabric. A hoop is handy for this, if you can't keep the thread loose enough.

FINISHING THE PILLOW

5. Neaten thread ends by trimming to ¼", and remove all marking lines. Block and press pillow front (see page 21).
6. Keeping design centered, trim pillow front to 15" square.
7. With right sides facing, stitch the front and back together, taking a ½" seam allowance and following the instructions on pages 48–49 for the type of backing you chose.
8. Stuff with pillow insert.

I felted this yard-sale find to get beautifully thick and textured fabric to stitch on. Formerly a woman's wool coat, it didn't give me very large pieces to work with, so I used a non-standard size for my pillow and stuffed it with polyester fill instead of a pillow insert. In my design, the little check becomes a backdrop to a flower spray reminiscent of Jacobean needlework. You could substitute traditional cotton check and stitch with cotton floss for a cheerful, summery pillow.

FINISHED SIZE: 10" x 13"

FABRICS

⅜ yard felted, checked, wool fabric or checked cotton, for pillow front

⅜ yard cotton fabric, for pillow back

THREAD

One 8-yard, 3-ply skein *each* of dark brown, light green, orange, coral, and yellow Persian wool

I used Paternayan, Coffee Brown/420, Loden Green/693, Spice/850, Strawberry/953, and Sunrise/815.

NOTIONS

Size 20 chenille needle

Small amount of cotton, wool, or polyester fill, for stuffing

STITCHES

A Chain Stitch (page 25)

B French Knot (page 26)

C Needleweaving (page 23)

D Satin Stitch (page 29)

E Stem Stitch (page 31)

PREPARING THE PILLOW FRONT AND BACK

1. Measure and cut a 13" × 16" rectangle from the felted wool for the pillow front (see page 44).
2. Measure and cut the pillow back fabric for a non-removable cover for a 10" × 13" pillow. Set pillow back aside.
3. Use a photocopier to enlarge the Checks with Crewel Flowers pattern on page 183 by 333%. With the pillow held "portrait" style (narrow edges at top and bottom), center the motif between the long sides, with the bottom of the flower stem 1½" up from the edge. (For advice on centering, see page 18.) Use the tracing paper method to transfer the design to the fabric (see page 19). Immediately draw over the motif with a water-soluble or child's washable marker.

STITCHING THE DESIGN

4. Using a single strand of dark brown wool, work the outline of the leaves and flowers in Stem Stitch.
5. **Stems and leaves.** Using a single strand of light green wool, work tightly packed Stem Stitch for the three stems and the two leaves.
6. **Left Flower.** Using a single strand of orange wool, fill the outer two sections of the flower with tightly packed Chain

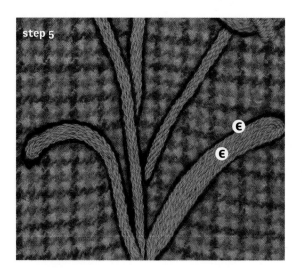

step 5

Stitch. Using two strands of yellow wool, fill the center two sections of the flower with Satin Stitch. Using two strands of coral wool, fill the top of the flower with Satin Stitch. Using two strands of light green wool, fill the bottom of the flower with Satin Stitch.

7. **Center Flower.** Using a double strand of orange wool, fill the outer ring of the flower with Satin Stitch. Work these stitches so they radiate from the center, like spokes on a bike. Using two strands of yellow wool, fill the center of the flower with tightly packed French Knots. Using a single strand of coral wool, work the middle ring of the flower in tightly packed Chain Stitch, working in a spiral fashion. (See page 61.)

8. **Right Flower.** Using a single strand of coral wool, fill the outer ring with tightly packed Chain Stitch. Using two strands of yellow wool, work the middle ring in Satin Stitch, packed tightly together. Work these stitches so they radiate from the center like the spokes on a bike wheel. Using two strands of orange wool, fill the center of the flower with tightly packed French Knots. Using two strands of light green wool, work three Needleweaving bars evenly placed around the center of the flower.

FINISHING THE PILLOW

9. Neaten the thread ends by trimming to ¼", and remove all marking lines. Block and press the pillow front (see page 21). Press from the wrong side, with the stitching face down on a terry cloth towel.

10. Trim the pillow front to 11" × 14", taking care to keep the design centered (see page 47).

11. With right sides facing, stitch the front and back together, taking a ½" seam and following the instructions on page 49 for a pillow with a non-removable cover.

12. Stuff with cotton, wool, or polyester fill.

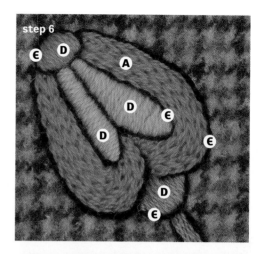

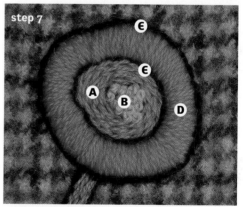

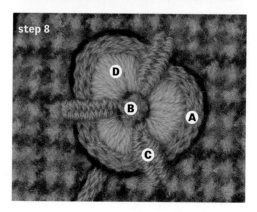

plaid pillow with flowers

I found this orange plaid wool remnant at the Brimfield (Massachusetts) Flea Market. It's an incredibly fine-woven wool kilt fabric in a pattern called "Antique MacGregor." I also found some blue plaid kilt fabric that I'll make into a coordinating pillow. I think the bold, circular flowers and sculpted leaves look fabulous against the loud plaid ground fabric. This floral design would look equally nice on other plaids, stripes, or even a plain linen ground fabric.

FINISHED SIZE: 15" x 15"

FABRICS

⅝ yard orange plaid fabric, for the pillow front

⅝ yard cotton fabric, for pillow back

THREAD

One 8-yard, 3-ply skein *each* of dark brown, chartreuse, bright orange, dull orange, bright yellow, and dark yellow Persian wool

I used Paternayan, Coffee Brown/420, Christmas Green/698, Spice/853, Ginger/883, Sunny Yellow/770, and Mustard/712.

NOTIONS

Size 20 chenille needle

14" x 14" square pillow insert (preferably down)

Small amount of cotton, wool, or polyester fill to pouf out the corners (my 15" pillow is a non-standard size)

STITCHES

Stem Stitch (page 25)

Chain Stitch (page 26)

French Knot (page 29)

Needleweaving (page 31)

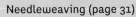

PREPARING THE FRONT AND BACK

1. For the pillow front, mark the center point of the plaid (see Centering Plaids, (page 95) then measure 9" out from that point in all four directions to mark your cutting lines for an 18" square. Cut along the weave of the fabric.
2. Measure and cut the pillow back fabric for either a non-removable cover or a flapped back opening for a 15" square pillow. (See page 48.) Set pillow back aside.
3. Use a photocopier to enlarge the Plaid Pillow with Flowers pattern on page 183 by 500%. Use the tracing paper method to transfer the design to the pillow front fabric, taking care to center the design on the fabric. Immediately draw over the motif with a water-soluble or child's washable marker. (See page 19 for advice on enlarging and copying patterns.)

STITCHING THE DESIGN

4. Using one strand of dark brown, work Stem Stitch around the edges of the outer and inner circles of each of the flowers.

working odd shapes

To work an odd shape, weave until you fill the widest area of threads, then continue with the reduced number until all are filled. You can weave over any number of threads, in any configuration.

5. **Flowers.** Using a single strand of wool, fill the inner and outer circles of each flower with tightly packed Chain Stitch. (Do not use Chain Stitch for the centers of the flowers.) Begin at the inner edge of each circle and work in spiral fashion to the outer edge. (See page 61.) Don't worry when the fabric becomes distorted; it will flatten out when you block it.

6. **Flower Centers.** Using two strands of wool, fill the center of each flower with tightly packed French Knots.

7. **Leaves.** The leaves are worked in Needleweaving Stitch with two strands of chartreuse wool. The pattern indicates the position of each leaf. When working the stitch, begin at the bottom part of the leaf and take care not to catch the base fabric with the green yarn, as illustrated on page 31. When you run out of yarn, bring the end to the back of the fabric and make a stitched knot to fasten it off. Begin the next strand where you left off. Although this attaches the leaf to the fabric, the leaf won't lose its sculptural quality. Some of the leaf tips extend beyond the main section of the leaf. When you have filled the shorter base threads, simply continue weaving over the longer ones that are not yet covered. (See illustration on facing page.)

FINISHING THE PILLOW

8. Neaten the thread ends by trimming to ¼", and remove all marking lines. Block and press the pillow front face down on a terry cloth towel (see page 21). You will need to spritz a lot of water on the flowers to get them to flatten out, but try not to press too hard on the leaves or they will lose their sculptural quality.

9. Trim the pillow front to 16" square, taking care to keep the design centered.

10. With right sides facing, stitch the front and back together, taking a ½" seam and following the instructions on pages 48–49 for the type of backing you chose.

11. Stuff with pillow insert and cotton, wool, or polyester fill.

centering plaids

Depending on the plaid you find, it's necessary to cut your piece so that the plaid will be centered on the pillow. You'll notice that you have several options for which part of the plaid you feel makes the strongest center point: It may be a point where horizontal and vertical stripes intersect, or it may be that you prefer to use an open portion of the plaid as the center. It's a subjective choice, and entirely up to you.

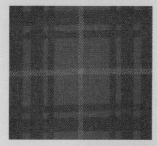

Porch Pillows

W hen I found the striped ground fabrics for these pillows, they reminded me of the fabric my grandmother used on her old wicker furniture on the sunporch at her house in New Jersey. Most embroidery is done on solid-colored fabrics, but I think stitching on patterned fabrics adds interest and beauty. I've chosen both bold and modest stripes for this set of pillows and decorated them in different ways to complement the base design.

mini-stripes and flowers

The all-over mini-stripe on this fabric makes a charming background for a loose, informal floral design. Choose colors that contrast well with the colors of the base stripes.

FINISHED SIZE: 12" x 18"

FABRICS

½ yard cotton fabric, with ⅜"-wide stripes, for the pillow front

½ yard cotton fabric, for the pillow back

THREAD

One 8.7-yard, 6-strand skein *each* of three colors of cotton embroidery floss

I used DMC 350 (rust) and 3848 (teal green), and Anchor 87 (magenta).

NOTIONS

Size 20 chenille needle

12" x 18" pillow insert (preferably down)

STITCHES

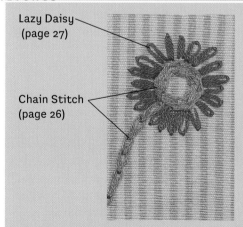

Lazy Daisy (page 27)

Chain Stitch (page 26)

PREPARING THE PILLOW FRONT AND BACK

1. Measure and cut a rectangle 15" × 21" wide from the striped cotton for the pillow front (see page 44).
2. Measure and cut the pillow back fabric for either a non-removable cover or a flapped back opening for a 12" × 18" pillow (see page 48). Set pillow back aside.
3. Use a photocopier to enlarge Mini-Stripes and Flowers pattern on page 183 by 333%. Using either the tracing paper method or the light table method, transfer the design to the fabric, taking care to center the motif. (For advice on centering, see page 19.)

STITCHING THE DESIGN

4. **Stems.** Using three strands of teal green cotton embroidery floss, work the stems in Chain Stitch.
5. **Flower Centers.** Using three strands of rust floss, work two rounds of chain stitch close together to outline the flower center.
6. **Flower Petals.** Using three strands of magenta floss, work Lazy Daisy Stitch around the flower centers. It isn't necessary for the petals to be perfect. The flowers are more lifelike when they are unevenly spaced with slightly different-length petals.

FINISHING THE PILLOW

7. Neaten the thread ends by trimming to ¼", and remove all marking lines. Block and press the pillow front, as shown on page 21.
8. Trim the pillow front to 13" × 19", taking care to keep the design centered (see page 47).
9. With right sides facing, stitch the front and back together, taking a ½" seam allowance and following the instructions on pages 48–49 for the type of backing you chose.
10. Stuff with pillow insert.

not-so-lazy daisies

The wide stripes of this fabric are ideal for stitchery. Choose colors that contrast with the base stripe and coordinate with the undecorated stripe. You may not be able to find fabrics exactly like these, with stripes the same width, but don't be afraid to improvise on other patterns.

FINISHED SIZE: 18" x 18"

FABRICS

⅔ yard cotton fabric, with 4"-wide stripes, for pillow front

⅔ yard cotton fabric, for pillow back

THREAD

One 8.7-yard, 6-strand skein of cotton embroidery floss in *each* of three colors

I used DMC 900 (dark orange), 165 (light green), and 976 (dark gold).

NOTIONS

Size 20 chenille needle

Five coins (I used quarters.)

18" square pillow insert (preferably down)

STITCHES

Chain Stitch (page 26)

Lazy Daisy (page 27)

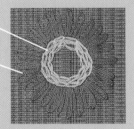

PREPARING THE PILLOW FRONT AND BACK

1. Measure and cut a 21" square from the cotton striped fabric for the pillow front (see page 44). Make sure you place the center of the stripe you will be embroidering at the center of the pillow.
2. Measure and cut the pillow back fabric for either a non-removable cover or a flapped back opening for an 18" square pillow (see page 48). Set pillow back aside.
3. Mark the mid-point of the fabric. Referring to the diagram on page 188, mark points 3" and 6" above and below the mid-point.
4. Place a coin at the center mark and on each of the other marks. Using a water-soluble or child's washable marker, trace around the outer edges of the coins.

STITCHING THE DESIGN

5. Using three strands of cotton embroidery floss, work two rounds of Chain Stitch along the circles you traced in step 4. I worked the center circle and the two outside circles in dark gold; the circles between these are worked in light green.
6. Using three strands of dark orange floss, work Lazy Daisy Stitch around the outside of each circle. As with the flowers on the Mini-Stripes and Flowers pillow (page 97), don't worry if your petals aren't perfect. A little uneven spacing and different-length petals make the flowers more lifelike.

FINISHING THE PILLOW

7. Neaten the thread ends by trimming to ¼", and remove all marking lines. Block and press the pillow front, as shown on page 21.
8. Trim the pillow front to 19" square, keeping the embroidered stripe and the center flower centered (see page 47).
9. With right sides facing, stitch the front and back together, taking a ½" seam allowance and following the instructions on pages 48–49 for the type of backing you chose.
10. Stuff with pillow insert.

undulating vines on stripes

Choose yarn colors that contrast well with the base stripe colors and coordinate with the alternating stripes, which are not embroidered.

FINISHED SIZE: 20" x 20"

FABRICS

¾ yard cotton fabric, with 3"-wide stripes, for pillow front

¾ yard cotton fabric, for pillow back

THREAD

One 8-yard, 3-ply skein of Persian wool in *each* of two colors

I used Paternayan, Loden Green/692 and Tobacco/742.

NOTIONS

Size 20 chenille needle

20" square pillow insert (preferably down)

STITCHES

Fern Stitch (page 25)

Bullion Knot (page 29)

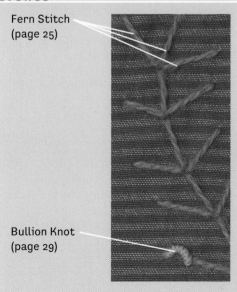

PREPARING THE PILLOW FRONT AND BACK

1. Measure and cut a 23" square from the cotton striped fabric for the pillow front (see page 44). Make sure you place the center of the middle stripe at the center of the square.
2. Measure and cut the pillow back fabric for either a non-removable cover or a flapped back opening for a 20" square pillow (see page 48). Set pillow back aside.
3. Referring to the diagram on page 184, use a see-through ruler and a water-soluble or child's washable marker to draw guidelines for the vine, as follows: Draw a line along the lengthwise centerline of each of the stripes on which you will be embroidering, then draw secondary lines ¾" from this centerline on each side of it. Draw an undulating line the length of each stripe within these guidelines. (See pattern on page 184.)

STITCHING THE DESIGN

4. Using one strand of loden green wool, work Fern Stitch along the undulating line. Vary the length of the fronds so that the line looks organic and natural.
5. Using one strand of light brown wool, create flower buds by working Bullion Knots at the ends of some of the stems. Space the flower buds randomly.

FINISHING THE PILLOW

6. Neaten the thread ends by trimming to ¼", and remove all marking lines. Block and press the pillow front, as shown on page 21.
7. Keeping the middle wide strip centered, trim the pillow front to 21" square.
8. With right sides facing, stitch the front and back together, taking a ½" seam allowance and following the instructions on pages 48–49 for the type of backing you chose.
9. Stuff with pillow insert.

Velvet Bugs

As a gardener, I'm continually amazed by the fascinating variety of bugs I find when I'm down on my knees weeding or digging in the soil. I'm not the first stitcher to be interested: Insects have been a favorite embroidery motif for hundreds of years. Bees, for example, were considered to be regal and so were often stitched in real gold and silk threads on the ornate clothing of French royalty. I thought it would be fun to embroider bugs on a luxurious fabric — velvet — as my take on these historic embroidered costumes. For my subjects, I chose a lowly moth, an elegant dragonfly, and a quirky walking stick.

Velvet is a little tricky to stitch and draw on. (For some tips, see A Velvet Touch, page 103.) If you're a true beginner, choose an easier ground fabric, such as linen or cotton, for this project. I backed my pillows with beautiful taffeta and striped silk fabrics to complement the dressy velvet.

dragonfly pillow

The dragonfly's outline is stitched in Persian wool; its body, head, and wings are worked in cotton embroidery floss. The sheen of the floss evokes flight and the transparency of the insect's luminescent wings.

FINISHED SIZE: 14" x 14"

FABRICS

½ yard of peach cotton velvet fabric, for pillow front

½ yard silk fabric, for pillow back

THREAD

One 8.7-yard, 6-strand skein of cotton embroidery floss *each* in chartreuse and aqua, and one 8-yard skein of 3-ply Persian wool in dark brown

For the floss, I used Anchor, 168 (aqua) and 280 (chartreuse); for the wool, I used Paternayan, Coffee Brown/420.

NOTIONS

Size 20 chenille needle

14" square pillow insert (preferably down)

STITCHES

Stem Stitch (page 25)

French Knot (page 29)

Laid Stitch (page 30)

Satin Stitch (page 23)

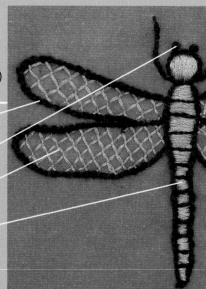

PREPARING THE PILLOW FRONT AND BACK

1. Measure and cut a 17" square from the velvet fabric for the pillow front (see page 144).
2. Measure and cut the pillow back fabric for either a non-removable cover or a flapped back opening for a 14" square pillow (see page 48). Set pillow back aside.
3. Using a photocopier, enlarge the Dragonfly Pillow pattern on page 184 by 200%. Using the tracing paper method, transfer the design to the fabric, centering the motif (see page 18). Retrace with a water-soluble or child's washable marker.

STITCHING THE DESIGN

4. **Outlines.** Using one strand of dark brown wool, outline dragonfly in Stem Stitch. Make the eyes with French Knots.
5. **Wings.** Using three strands of chartreuse cotton floss, fill the wings with Laid Stitch, worked diagonally.
6. **Head and Body.** Using six strands of aqua cotton floss, work the head in Satin Stitch. Work the striped body in alternating Satin Stitch bands of chartreuse (six strands) and aqua cotton floss. Using one strand of dark brown wool, work one Satin Stitch between each band of color on the body to separate the aqua and chartreuse stripes.

FINISHING THE PILLOW

7. Neaten the thread ends by trimming to ¼", and remove all marking lines. Block and press the pillow front (see page 21). Press from the wrong side, and avoid pressing too hard on the fabric and crushing the pile (see A Velvet Touch, facing page).
8. Trim the pillow front to 15" square, taking care to keep the design centered (see page 47).
9. With right sides facing, stitch the front and back together, taking a ½" seam allowance and following the instructions on pages 48–49 for the type of backing you chose.
10. Stuff with pillow insert.

Available in both interior-decorating and dress-fabric departments and stores, velvet is made in cotton, silk, rayon, and mohair. The pile or nap of velvet creates the soft, luxurious texture that makes you want to stroke it. In spite of its elegance, it is very durable and so is often a choice for upholstery. Make sure you test the fabric with your needle and thread before stitching on it, as some velvets are very densely woven and may therefore prove too difficult to use as a ground fabric for stitchery. Here are some other tips for working with velvets:

✱ Velvets with a gluelike backing are often found in interior-decorating stores. Avoid these, as they are too difficult to stitch on.

✱ Prewash velvet fabric in the washing machine and dry it in the dryer. This makes it softer and more supple to stitch on. Avoid wrinkles by taking the fabric out of the dryer as soon as it stops running.

✱ When marking velvet, use the tracing paper method. Immediately after removing the pattern, trace over the design with a water-soluble or child's washable marker. Tracing lines do not last on the pile of the fabric.

✱ Avoid using an embroidery hoop on velvet because it crushes the pile. It is pretty impossible to restore the original look once the velvet is marred in this way.

✱ Stitch carefully and neatly. If you have to rip out embroidery on velvet, you will inevitably remove some of the pile along with your stitches. The resulting holes cannot be repaired.

✱ When blocking your finished stitchery, place a folded bath towel on your ironing board and place the stitched piece face down on the towel so that you can steam press it from the wrong side. Avoid pressing too hard, or you will flatten the pile.

A Velvet Touch

moth pillow

I worked the moth entirely in wool yarns to give it the soft, fluffy look most moths really have.

FINISHED SIZE: 16" x 16"

FABRICS

⅝ yard moss green cotton velvet, for pillow front

⅝ yard silk fabric, for pillow back

THREADS

One 8-yard, 3-ply skein *each* of dark brown, aqua, and peach Persian wool

I used Paternayan, Coffee Brown/420, Teal Blue/522, and Ginger/883.

NOTIONS

Size 20 chenille needle

16" square pillow insert (preferably down)

STITCHES

Stem Stitch
(page 25)

Satin Stitch
(page 23)

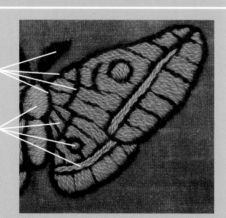

PREPARING THE PILLOW FRONT AND BACK

1. Measure and cut a 19" square from the velvet for the pillow front (see page 44).
2. Measure and cut the pillow back fabric for either a non-removable cover or a flapped back opening for a 16" square pillow (see page 48). Set pillow back aside.
3. Use a photocopier to enlarge the Moth Pillow pattern on page 184 by 167%. Using the tracing paper method, transfer the design to the fabric, centering it (see page 18.) Immediately draw over the design with a water-soluble or child's washable marker.

STITCHING THE DESIGN

Note: Use one strand of Persian wool throughout.

4. **Outlines.** Using dark brown, outline moth in Stem Stitch.
5. **Head and Antennae.** Using dark brown, work head in Satin Stitch. Work antennae in closely packed Stem Stitch.
6. **Wings.** Using dark brown, outline wings and inner circles and other wing patterns with Stem Stitch. Using aqua, fill centers of circles with Satin Stitch; fill horizontal wing stripes with Stem Stitch, closely packed together. Using peach wool, fill in remaining areas of the wings with Stem Stitch, closely packed together.
7. **Body.** Using aqua, fill body with Satin Stitch.

FINISHING THE PILLOW

8. Neaten thread ends by trimming to ¼", and remove all marking lines. Block and press pillow front (see page 21). Press from wrong side, and avoid pressing too hard on fabric and crushing pile (see A Velvet Touch, page 103).
9. Trim pillow front to 17" square, keeping design centered (see page 47).
10. With right sides facing, stitch front and back together, taking a ½" seam allowance and following instructions on pages 48–49 for the type of backing you chose.
11. Stuff with pillow insert.

walking stick

*Because the walking stick is such a sturdy bug,
I felt wool was the most appropriate thread for it.*

FINISHED SIZE: 16" x 16"

FABRICS

⅝ yard aqua cotton velvet, for pillow front

⅝ yard silk fabric, for pillow back

THREADS

One 8-yard, 3-ply skein each of dark brown, chartreuse, and melon Persian wool

I used Paternayan, Coffee Brown/420, Olive Green/652, and Copper/862.

NOTIONS

Size 20 chenille needle

16" square pillow insert (preferably down)

STITCHES

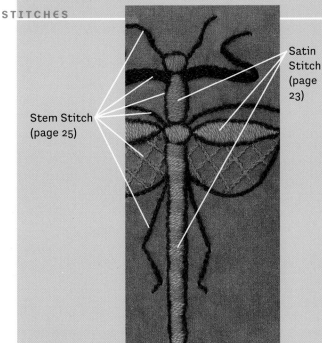

Satin Stitch (page 23)

Stem Stitch (page 25)

PREPARING THE PILLOW FRONT AND BACK

1. Measure and cut a 19" square from the velvet pillow front fabric (see page 44).
2. Measure and cut the pillow back fabric for either a non-removable cover or a flapped back opening for a 16" square pillow (see page 48). Set pillow back aside.
3. Using a photocopier, enlarge the Walking Stick pattern on page 185 by 250%. Using tracing paper method, transfer design to fabric, centering the design. Immediately draw over the motif with a water-soluble or child's washable marker.

STITCHING THE DESIGN

4. Using one strand of brown, work the outlines, antennae, and front and back legs of the walking stick in Stem Stitch. (Closely pack the Stem Stitches for the front legs.)
5. **Wings.** Using two strands of copper, work the top interior curved shapes in Satin Stitch. Using one strand of olive green, work the diagonal plaid in Stem Stitch.
6. **Body.** Using two strands of olive green, work the head and upper body in Satin Stitch. Using two strands of copper, work the center body circle in Satin Stitch.
7. **Tail.** Using two strands of copper or olive green, work alternate stripes of the tail in Satin Stitch.

FINISHING THE PILLOW

8. Neaten thread ends by trimming to ¼", and remove all marking lines. Block and press pillow front (see page 21). Press from wrong side, and avoid pressing too hard on fabric and crushing pile (see A Velvet Touch, at page 103).
9. Trim the pillow front to 17" square, taking care to keep the design centered (see page 47).
10. With right sides facing, stitch the front and back together, taking a ½" seam allowance, and following the instructions on pages 48–49 for the type of backing you chose.
11. Stuff with pillow insert.

Kitchen Stitchin'

The mail gets dropped on the kitchen counter, the Sunday paper gets read, homework is done, meals are prepared (even if that means just opening take-out containers), dishes are washed and dried, and, late at night, friends solve the world's problems after a casual dinner and a good bottle of wine. A kitchen envelops the folks who share the space with love, warmth, and sustenance. What a perfect place to express your newfound creativity with stitchery!

Embroidery has a long history of decorating the kitchen. Visit any flea market or antique store, and you'll find hand-stitched tea towels, tablecloths, and napkins. Old-fashioned Cross-Stitch samplers with silly sayings used to grace most kitchen walls. Sure it's nice to buy vintage needlework, but it's just as nice (maybe even nicer) to make it yourself. You'll find lots of ideas for stitching for your kitchen in this chapter, many of which are old-fashioned ones that I've re-interpreted for the modern home. They're all useful and sure to bring a smile. Most take only an evening to whip up, and all make welcome gifts to any friend lucky enough to receive them.

Going Dotty Tea Cozy

Tea cozies have taken their share of knocks, but as far as I am concerned, it's time for a revival of this completely useful object, which can also add a bright spot to any kitchen scene. One of my family's favorite wintertime activities is sharing a pot of Yorkshire Gold tea among the three of us and friends. When we have time, we make a batch of oat scones with wild blueberries to go with the tea (see page 111). There's no more-perfect way to spend a snowy Sunday afternoon! Keeping a pot of tea hot in winter can be a challenge, though, because it cools down so quickly; so a tea cozy is absolutely necessary if you're going to get a hot second cup. I've knitted fanciful tea cozies, but embroidery is so much quicker.

A tea cozy — along with a beautiful teapot and a tea tin full of your favorite brew — makes a great wedding present. Although your friends may not have discovered the luxury of a winter afternoon tea party, they'll be eager to try it out.

tea cozy

For the fabric, I felted a blanket in the washing machine, then used four layers of it, so the cozy keeps tea piping hot for several hours. The cozy is generously sized to fit a largish pot. The colorful, playful polka dots feature one of my favorite stitches — Spider Web. I used Persian wool yarn for the stitching, but worsted-weight wool knitting yarn would be fine. I used contrasting color lining fabric for a surprise element.

FINISHED SIZE: 11" high x 15" wide

FABRIC

1 yard recycled, washed, and felted wool blanket, sweater, or coating fabric; or ½ yard *each* of two different colors, for contrasting cozy and lining

THREAD

One 8-yard skein *each* of 3-ply Persian wool in five colors for the dots and two skeins for the Blanket Stitch edging

I used Paternayan, Butterscotch/702, Christmas Green/697, Caribbean Blue/592, and Hot Pink/962 for the dots and Periwinkle/341 for the edging.

NOTIONS

Size 18 chenille needle

Coins of several sizes, to use as templates for the circles (I used pennies, nickels, dimes, and quarters.)

⅓ yard buckram or other stiff interfacing (available at sewing stores)

Fabric glue

STITCHES

Blanket Stitch (page 26)

Spider Web Stitch (page 31)

PREPARING THE FABRIC

1. Wash and felt your fabric, if you haven't already done so. (See page 46.)
2. Use a photocopier to enlarge the pattern for the Tea Cozy on page 189 by 500%. Cut around the template. With the template pinned to the wool fabric, cut four pieces all the same color, or if you want a contrasting lining, cut two pieces in one color and two pieces in a second color.
3. Using the same pattern, cut two pieces of the buckram.
4. Lay one of the pieces for the outer layer on a flat surface. Randomly place 10 coins on the piece until you get an arrangement you like. Using a water-soluble or child's washable marker, trace around the coins.
5. Repeat step 4 on another outer piece for the other side.

STITCHING THE DESIGN

6. Using three plies of wool, work Spider Web Stitch on nine spokes over one of the circles. Work each of the circles in the same stitch, using the five different colors randomly to your liking, or follow my design. Repeat on the other outer layer.

FINISHING THE COZY

8. Block both embroidered pieces. Press, placing the embroidered side face down on a terry cloth towel and using a good spritz of water. (See page 21.)
9. Trim ¾" off the edge all the way around the buckram pieces.
10. Apply fabric glue lightly to the wrong side of one of the embroidered pieces, stopping 1" away from the edge all around. Center the buckram on top of the glue. Lay the lining piece on top of the buckram, aligning the edges with the embroidered piece beneath. Repeat with the each of the layers for the other side. Place a book on top of each piece to keep the pieces flat and in contact with each other until the glue is dry. Let stand overnight.
11. Using two plies of periwinkle wool, work Blanket Stitch along the straight edge of one of the glued-together pieces

(see page 26). Space the stitches about ½" apart, and make the "legs" about ½" long. Repeat on the other piece.

12. With lining sides facing and embroidered sides to outside, pin the two pieces together, aligning edges. If edges are not even, trim to neaten. Using two plies of periwinkle wool, work three Blanket Stitches at one of the corners, going into the fabric at the same point for each stitch (see page 26). Take care to go neatly through all layers. This stitching attaches the front to the back and also turns the corner neatly in Blanket Stitch. Continue to use Blanket Stitch along the entire curved edge, ending at the other corner with three stitches done in the same manner. When you run out of yarn, sandwich your knot on the inside (see page 158).

13. Neaten the thread ends by trimming to ¼", and remove all marking lines. Block the cozy to neaten the Blanket Stitch.

14. Enjoy a warm pot of tea all afternoon.

my favorite oat scones

1½ cups all-purpose flour
1¼ cups rolled oats
¼ cup granulated sugar
1 tablespoon baking powder
1 teaspoon cream of tartar
½ teaspoon salt
⅔ cup butter, melted and cooled
⅓ cup milk
1 egg
1½ cups blueberries, fresh or frozen (if frozen, do not thaw before using)

1. Preheat the oven to 425°F. Grease a cookie sheet.

2. Combine the flour, rolled oats, sugar, baking powder, cream of tartar, and salt in a large mixing bowl.

3. Add the cooled butter, milk, and egg to the dry ingredients. Mix until just moistened. Stir in the frozen blueberries. The dough will be moist.

4. Shape the dough into an 8-inch circle on the greased cookie sheet. With a long knife, cut the circle into 8 wedges, to create the classic triangular shape. (Do not separate the wedges.)

5. Bake in the middle of the oven for 12 to 15 minutes, until they are golden brown. (Use a cake tester to check: If it comes out clean, they're done.)

6. Serve the scones warm, with a fresh pot of tea.

a good-egg cozy

As the saying goes, everything old is new again! Reminiscent of times gone by, egg cozies speak of domestic bliss. If you have overnight weekend guests, surprise them by serving toast, a pot of tea, and soft-boiled eggs, topped with these quirky chick-inspired egg cozies. A whole set of covered egg cups makes for a memorable, and leisurely, Sunday morning breakfast.

My egg cozies are made of felted wool blankets and sweaters in a variety of colors. For fun, I like to make each side a different color. This project is a great way to use up your scraps, and it's a sort of mini-version of the larger, more complex tea cozy.

FINISHED SIZE: 3½" long x 4" wide

FABRIC

Small scraps of recycled, washed, and felted wool blanket, sweater, or coating fabric in fun colors

THREAD

One 8-yard skein of 3-ply Persian wool

I used Paternayan, Coffee Brown/420.

NOTIONS

Size 20 chenille needle

STITCHES

Backstitch
(page 24)

Blanket Stitch
(page 26)

French Knot
(page 29)

Satin Stitch
(page 23)

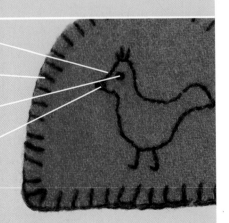

PREPARING THE FABRIC

1. Wash and felt your fabric, if you haven't already done it. (See page 46.)

2. Use a photocopier to enlarge the A Good-Egg Cozy pattern on page 189 by 200%. Use the tracing paper method to transfer the design to the felted fabric, and cut out two pieces (a back and a front) for each egg cozy.

3. Use the tracing paper method to transfer the chicken design to the piece for the front. Go over the traced lines with a water-soluble or child's washable marker to make them more visible.

STITCHING THE DESIGN

Use one ply of wool throughout.

4. Work the outline of the chicken in Backstitch.

5. Work a French Knot for the eye.

6. Fill the beak with Satin Stitch.

7. Work Blanket Stitch across the straight edge of the front and back pieces of the cozy.

8. With wrong sides facing, pin the front and back pieces together. Follow the Tea Cozy directions (page 111, step 12) for working Blanket Stitch around corners and along edges.

FINISHING THE COZY

9. Neaten the thread ends by trimming to ¼", and remove all marking lines. Block. (See page 21.)

10. Make a soft-boiled egg, put it in an egg cup, and top it with a cozy. Enjoy!

Pressed for Time

Years after my first trip to Paris, I still love French roast coffee made in a French press coffeepot. To keep it hot, I designed a very simple, small wool felt cozy with Velcro closures to go around the pot. The thick, felted wool helps to keep the coffee hot for that second cup I always need in the morning.

coffee cozy

My cozy fits the most popular medium-sized French press. If your press is larger, wrap a paper pattern around the pot to determine the size needed for the fabric

FINISHED SIZE: 12½" x 5¾" (fits a medium-sized French press pot)

FABRIC

Recycled, washed, and felted wool blanket, sweater, or coating fabric

THREAD

One 8-yard, 3-ply skein *each* of Persian wool in three colors

I used Paternayan, Dark Brown/420, Christmas Green/697, and Caribbean Blue/590.

NOTIONS

Size 20 chenille needle

3" piece of Velcro

Fabric glue

STITCHES

Blanket Stitch (page 26)

Fern Stitch (page 25)

Backstitch (page 24)

French Knot (page 29)

Lazy Daisy (page 27)

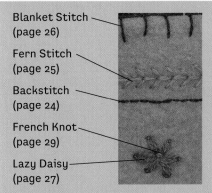

PREPARING THE FABRIC

1. Wash and felt your fabric, if you haven't already done so (see page 46).
2. From the felted wool, cut two pieces 12½" × 5¾" for the cozy and two pieces 2" × 2¾" for the tab closure.
3. On one of the cozy pieces, use a water-soluble or child's washable marker to draw your stitching guidelines, referring to the diagram on page 190: two parallel lines, 1¼" and 1¾" in from each of the long sides (four lines in all), and seven marks aligned along the centerline lengthwise and spaced 1½" apart, with the middle dot centered on the piece (see page 18).

STITCHING THE DESIGN

Use a single ply of wool throughout.

5. With green, work along the two outer lines in Fern Stitch.
6. With brown, work along the two inner lines in Backstitch.
7. At each of the seven dots, make blue Lazy Daisy flowers. Make a single green French Knot in the center of each flower.
8. Pin together the embroidered piece and the second cozy piece, with wrong sides facing.
9. At the center at each end, sandwich one of the tabs between the two layers, so that the ends of the tabs extend ½" into the cozy. Pin them in place.
10. Using brown, work Blanket Stitch around entire cozy. To hide knots and ends, sandwich them between the layers (see page 158). Work three stitches at each corner to turn (see page 26). Work the Blanket Stitch through each tab (see page 117).

FINISHING THE COZY

11. Neaten the thread ends by trimming to ¼", and remove all marking lines. Block the cozy, using a steam iron to even out the stitching. (See page 21.)
12. Use fabric glue to attach one piece of Velcro (smooth side facing the fabric) to the outside of one of the tabs and the other piece to the inside of the other tab.
13. Make yourself a nice hot pot of coffee.

The Best Potholders — Ever

Potholders made from felted wool are the bees' knees! Two layers of re-cycled, felted wool blankets or wool sweaters make it impossible to burn your-self. Wool potholders can be machine-washed when they get gunky, because the felted fabric has been pre-shrunk. And, wool is naturally flame resistant. I like to cut out a bunch of potholders, then tuck the pieces along with yarn and needles into a little bag so I have an easy project on hand when talk-ing on the phone or visiting with friends.

You can stitch a pair of these in less than an hour. Stitch on a saying ("hot, hot, hot" or "If you can't take the heat. . .") or just work Blanket Stitch edging and leave the middle plain; they'll still be cute.

FINISHED SIZE: 7½" circles and 7½" and 8½" squares

FABRIC

Various small pieces of wool blankets or wool sweaters, felted and dyed in fun colors

THREAD

One 8-yard, 3-ply skein of dark brown Persian wool; or odds and ends of worsted-weight wool knitting yarn

I used Paternayan, Coffee Brown/420.

NOTIONS

Size 20 chenille needle

One 7½" salad plate, as a template for the circular potholder

STITCHES

French Knot
(page 29)

Lazy Daisy
(page 27)

Straight Stitch
(page 24)

Blanket Stitch
(page 26)

PREPARING THE FABRIC

1. Cut two pieces (see sizes at left) for each potholder: one color for back and one for front. (Trace a salad plate for circle.)
2. Cut a hanging loop ⅝" by 4" in a third color.

STITCHING THE DESIGN

3. Decorate front or both sides with any of the following motifs:
   - Four or five Lazy Daisy flowers, randomly spaced
   - Straight Stitch around a point to form a five-pointed star
   - French Knots, randomly spaced
4. Pin pieces together, wrong sides facing. Fold loop in half and pin it between the two layers at a corner or anywhere along circle. Allow ends of loop to extend about ½" into potholder.
5. Use Blanket Stitch to attach the two pieces. When you get to the loop, stitch through all three layers (see below). Work three stitches at each corner to turn (see page 26).

FINISHING THE POTHOLDERS

6. Neaten the thread ends by trimming to ¼", and remove all marking lines. Block (see page 21).

blanket stitch, interrupted

To work Blanket Stitch in two steps, poke the needle through all three layers of fabric, and pull the thread to the back of the work, keeping a loop at the front. Now return the needle to the front of the work by poking the needle through the middle layer only, neatly enclosing all three layers. Make sure you finish the Blanket Stitch on the front by catching the needle in the loop you left loose.

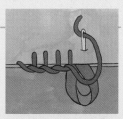

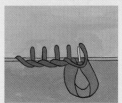

Ode to a Sunflower

My husband, Mark, and I have a thing for sunflowers. We grow a field full of rows and rows of different varieties on our farm. Last summer, I set up a little roadside stand where we sold them, so our neighbors could enjoy their beauty in their own homes. Every afternoon, my daughter and I picked armfuls and set them out in bouquets at the stand for the sunflower fairies. In the evenings, we collected the sunflower fairies' money. Our efforts make us thoroughly appreciate the work and care farmers put into their crops and roadside stands. Farming and needleworking have many things in common. The quest for the beautiful, most perfect sunflower is like perfecting an extraordinary piece of stitchery. Both require lots of love, care, and patience. When winter halts the sunflower harvest, we still enjoy their beauty stitched on our table linens.

sunflower tablecloth

I purchased my tablecloth and napkins ready-made at Crate and Barrel, but many other stores also carry nice-quality, pure-cotton napkins and tablecloths to decorate with your favorite motif. Look for bold, sunny colors that offset the bright colors of the stitchery. The napkin design would also be at home on a brightly colored dishtowel.

Although you can make each napkin in about 30 minutes, the tablecloth will take several hours. My tablecloth is square but you can use the same motifs on a rectangular, oval, or circular cloth.

FINISHED SIZE: 60" x 60"

FABRIC

Purchased cotton tablecloth in a sunny yellow color

THREAD

Three 8.7-yard, 6-strand skeins *each* of cotton embroidery floss in two colors and one skein *each* in two colors

I used three skeins each of DMC 900 (orange) and 3607 (hot pink) and one skein each of DMC 906 (green) and 3838 (periwinkle blue).

NOTIONS

Size 22 chenille needle

STITCHES

Chain Stitch (page 26)
French Knot (page 29)
Backstitch (page 24)
Straight Stitch (page 24)
Stem Stitch (page 25)
Fly Stitch (page 27)

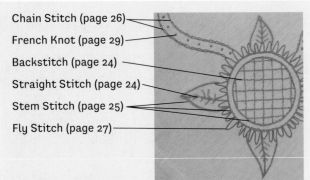

PREPARING THE FABRIC

1. Wash and dry the tablecloth to remove the sizing.
2. Use a photocopier to enlarge the Sunflower Tablecloth pattern on page 189 by 250%. Using light table method and a water-soluble or child's washable marker, transfer flower to each corner of cloth. Place bottom of leaves 4½" in each edge.
3. Referring to diagram on page 189, create guidelines for swirly border: With a water-soluble or child's washable marker and a see-through ruler, draw a line 7" in from all edges, connecting the four flowers. Draw a swooping double line that moves 1" above and below the straight line. If you aren't happy with the way your line swoops, spritz it to remove marks, let it dry, and try again. Draw lines ¼" from it, one above and one below it.

STITCHING THE DESIGN

Use three strands of embroidery floss throughout.

4. **Flower Center:**
   - With hot pink, work Stem Stitch on the two circles that form the flower center.
   - With periwinkle blue, work Backstitch to form the grid in the flower center.
5. **Petals.** With orange, work Fly Stitch for the petals around flower center. Make petals different widths and lengths.
6. **Leaves.** With bright green, work Stem Stitch along leaf outlines and center veins. (Begin each leaf just outside a stitched petal.) With same green, work lateral veins in Straight Stitch.
7. **Swirly Border:**
   - With orange, work French Knots every ½" along the middle guideline on all four sides.
   - With hot pink, work Chain Stitch along the two outer guidelines.

FINISHING THE TABLECLOTH

8. Neaten thread ends by trimming to ¼", and remove all marking lines. Block and press tablecloth (see page 21).

sunflower napkins

FINISHED SIZE: 18" x 18"

FABRIC

Purchased cotton napkins in yellow, hot pink, periwinkle, orange, green, and turquoise

THREAD

One 8.7-yard, 6-strand skein *each of cotton embroidery floss in five colors*

I used DMC 900 (orange), 3607 (hot pink), 906 (green), 3838 (periwinkle blue), and 742 (yellow).

NOTIONS

Size 18 chenille needle

STITCHES

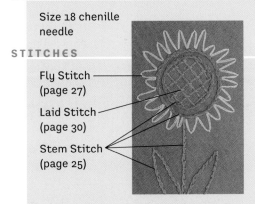

Fly Stitch (page 27)

Laid Stitch (page 30)

Stem Stitch (page 25)

PREPARING THE FABRIC

1. Wash and dry the napkins to remove sizing.
2. Use a photocopier to enlarge Sunflower Napkins pattern on page 189 by 167%. Using light table method and a water-soluble or child's washable marker, transfer design to one corner of each napkin at a diagonal, with stem end 2½" from edge.

STITCHING THE DESIGN

Choose your floss color to contrast with the color of the napkin. Use three strands of embroidery floss throughout.

3. **Flower Center.** Work Stem Stitch on the two circles that form the flower center. Work Laid Stitch to form the grid in the flower center.
4. **Petals.** Work Fly Stitch to create the petals around the outside of the flower. Make the petals different widths and lengths for a more natural look.
5. **Leaves and Stem.** Work Stem Stitch along the leaf outline and the flower stem.

FINISHING THE NAPKINS

6. Finish as for Sunflower Tablecloth.

friendship cloth

Janet Reynolds, co-owner of The Blue Bunny in Dedham, Massachusetts, covers her table with this cloth and asks her dinner guests to sign their names, which she later retraces in Stem Stitch. To start your own tradition, choose a nice crisp linen or linen-cotton. Supply your guests with a pencil or fine-point washable marker for signing. Work Stem Stitch or Backstitch in cotton floss. What a wonderful shower or wedding gift!

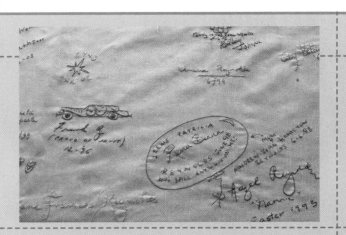

Dishtowels à la Française

My fascination for all things French began when I entered ninth grade. Fashion design was my career plan, so I chose French, the language of fashion, as my linguistic credit. One day I hoped to visit Paris, and it would be good to be able to ask *en français* for *les toilette*. My French teacher, Linda Lebo, was very chic. As a gawky ninth grader I aspired to be her one day. She wore short skirts and tight blouses (not the personal style I adopted) — I still remember her sassy stories of France!

That was a long time ago, and I've traveled to France many times since. I have an out-of-control collection of French cookbooks that I live through vicariously. My heroine, Julia Child, has taught me to cook some wonderful French meals. Mark and I named our daughter in part after this great lady. These towels are my homage to many a great French meal served with panache at small bistros throughout France.

bistro dishtowel

I love to collect dishtowels at specialty discount stores or in European markets. With their pretty striped or plaid patterns and nice soft cotton, they make a reasonably priced hostess gift and can even double as extra-large napkins.

FINISHED SIZE: 20" x 25"

FABRIC

Striped or solid-colored purchased cotton dishtowel, with border if available (I found mine at Crate and Barrel, but all home stores have lovely choices.)

THREAD

One 8.7-yard, 6-strand skein of cotton embroidery floss

I used Anchor 48 (dark blue).

NOTIONS

Size 20 chenille needle

STITCHES

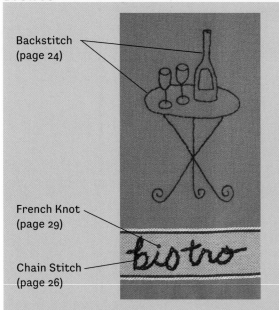

Backstitch (page 24)

French Knot (page 29)

Chain Stitch (page 26)

PREPARING THE FABRIC

1. Use a photocopier to enlarge the Bistro Dishtowel pattern on page 190 by 250%. Using the tracing paper method, transfer the design to the center of one end of the dishtowel. Retrace the lines with water-soluble or child's washable marker.

STITCHING THE DESIGN

Use three strands of embroidery floss throughout.

2. Work Backstitch to outline table, glasses, and bottle. Because a dishtowel gets heavy use, secure all knots carefully.

3. Work Chain Stitch along the lettering for the word *bistro*. Dot the letter i with a French Knot.

FINISHING THE DISHTOWEL

4. Wash the dishtowel to neaten the stitches and remove marking lines. Trim ends neatly and iron.

shopping for something new

Home stores carry pre-finished items in a wide range of lovely colors and patterns in up-to-date decorating styles just waiting for your stitchery. Look for cotton curtains, solid-color napkins, placemats, and tablecloths. Choose smooth fabrics, so the embroidery lies above the surface. Pure cotton or linen, or blends of cotton, linen, hemp, silk, and rayon are best. Make sure the fabric isn't too tightly woven. Bed sheets with 200 threads per inch are much easier to push a needle through than 400 thread-count sheets. At the end of winter, look for bargains in fringed wool and cashmere throws and blankets.

Café Julia dishtowel

Every home needs dozens of dishcloths: to sop up spills, polish silver or furniture, or just dry dishes. When you decorate them with embroidery, you turn them into items of unexpected whimsy. The rhythm of drying dishes is even more soothing when you're using a hand-embroidered towel.

FINISHED SIZE: 20" x 25"

FABRIC

Striped or solid-colored, purchased cotton dishtowel

THREAD

One 8.7-yard, 6-strand skein *each* of cotton embroidery floss in dark blue and gold.

I used Anchor 48 (dark blue) and 306 (gold).

NOTIONS

Size 18 chenille needle

STITCHES

French Knot (page 29)

Backstitch (page 24)

Lazy Daisy (page 27)

Chain Stitch (page 26)

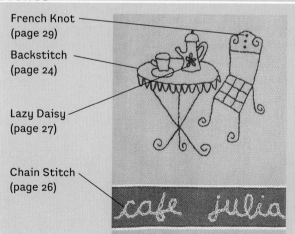

PREPARING THE FABRIC

1. Use a photocopier to enlarge the Café Julia dishtowel pattern on page 190 by 250%. Using the tracing paper method, transfer both designs to the center of one end of the dishtowel. Draw over the traced lines with a water-soluble or child's washable marker to make them more visible. Note: If you would like to personalize the name of the café, as I did, write the word *café* followed by the name of the café's owner in your best handwriting. Enlarge the lettering to the size needed, and transfer as above.

STITCHING THE DESIGN

Use three strands of embroidery floss throughout.

2. Work Backstitch to outline the table, chair, coffee pot, and cup and saucer. Because a dishtowel will get lots of use and be washed frequently, make sure all your beginning and ending knots are secure.

3. Work Lazy Daisy Stitch to create a flower in the middle of the coffee pot.

4. Work three stacked French Knots at the center back of the chair. Work a French Knot at the center of the flower and on the lid of the coffee pot.

5. Work the lettering in Chain Stitch. Dot the letters *i* and *j* with French Knots.

FINISHING THE DISHTOWEL

6. Wash the towel to neaten the stitches and remove marking lines. Trim the ends and iron.

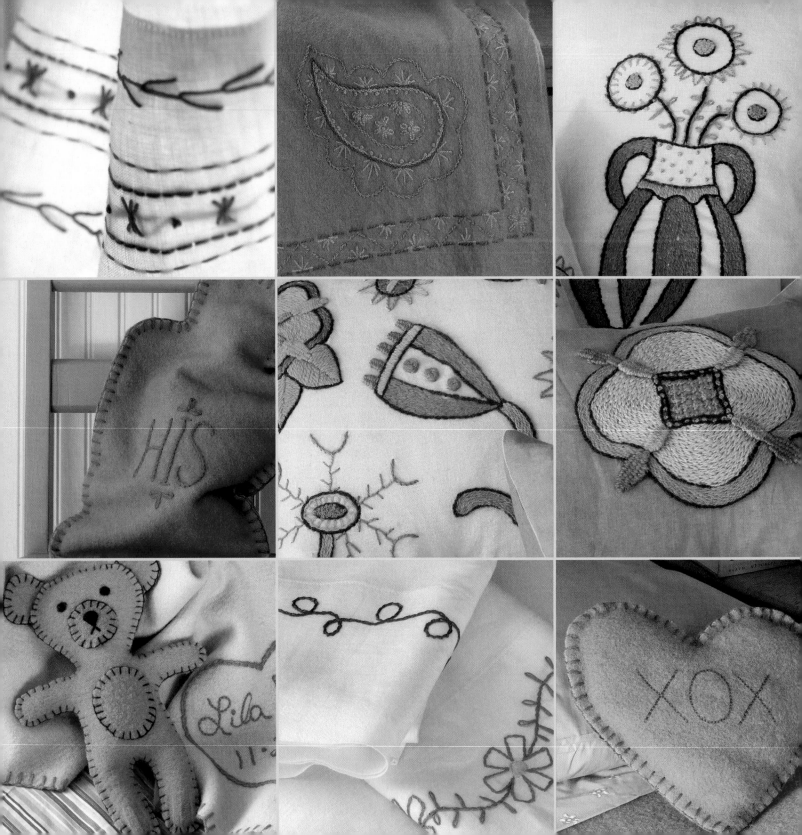

A Hand-Stitched Haven

The bedroom — it's a haven of peace, love, and slumber, and perfect for adorning with your own romantic, but modern, stitchery. For centuries, hand-stitched bed linens and other home textiles formed the basis of every dowry or hope chest, providing a valuable legacy of comfort and beauty for a young family's new home. This tradition may seem foreign and far away, but women who furnish a hope chest know something: Nothing is prettier than an object stitched by hand with love.

Most of the ideas here are completely old-fashioned — so old-fashioned they look new again. Many would make a perfect gift. From whimsical hot-water bottle covers to a romantic, heart-shaped pillow, there's something here for everyone — even a teddy bear for the small set. So, get stitching and creating your own modern version of those wonderful old textiles. Make yours quirky and off-beat by using your own favorite color combinations. Imagine awakening to your own curtains after sleeping on hand-stitched pillowcases — what could be better?

Gram's Pillowcases My Way

I have very fond childhood memories of sleepovers at my grandmother's house. I would sleep in my dad's old room. On the bed were crisp, white cotton pillowcases with edges decorated with beautiful embroidery. I remember staring at the beautifully stitched flowers and baskets in faded shades of cotton floss and wondering how they were made. Over the years since my grandmother died, I've built a career in needlework out of the interests my mother and grandmother nurtured in me. For years, I've longed to re-create those pillowcases I remember from my youth for my own home, but with a modern flair. Handmade and embroidered pillowcases make luxurious presents for both children and adults. Develop your own ideas for borders, including handwritten monograms or messages that personalize a set for someone you love.

my grandmother and great-grandmother lived together after both their husbands died. The family had come from Germany to America in 1911 to work in a hosiery factory in New Jersey, and they brought along their immaculate needlework skills. From my Gram, I learned that my hands should always be busy. I now know how extremely lucky I was to have had such a hard-working, talented role model in my life.

Gram and her German friends had a sewing circle every week at a different house. Every woman brought a basket filled with crochet, knitting, embroidery, quilting, or mending to work on while she visited with friends. If we were good, my sisters and I got to attend on Gram's week. I remember listening to the women talk and laugh. Every once in a while, they'd slip back into German when they wanted to talk about us or my mom or something they didn't want us to understand. For my sisters and I, the best part of the afternoon was the amazing coffee and *kuchen* they served.

I used to be sad that modern women had lost the tradition of getting together with their needlework projects, but now, with "stitch and bitch" and other groups springing up every-where, not only in private homes, but in yarn stores, bookstores, and even bars, it looks as if the idea is having a well-deserved rebirth.

GRAM'S APPLE KUCHEN

This is the cake my grandmother frequently made for her sewing circle. She used whatever fruit was in season — apples, peaches, plums, raspberries, or rhubarb. This recipe makes one smallish cake.

1 cup flour
1 teaspoon baking soda
½ teaspoon baking powder
¼ teaspoon salt
2 tablespoons butter, room temperature
¼ cup granulated sugar
1 large egg
1 teaspoon lemon zest
⅓ cup sour cream
2 large Granny Smith apples, peeled and sliced into ⅛" slices, or enough other in-season fruit to cover the pan generously
4 ounces almonds, sliced
5 tablespoons brown sugar
2 tablespoons flour
2 tablespoons butter, melted
½ teaspoon cinnamon
¼ teaspoon nutmeg

1. Mix and sift together the flour, baking soda, baking powder, and salt.

2. Using a mixer, cream the butter and sugar together until light colored. Add the egg, and beat until fluffy.

3. Add the dry ingredients to the creamed mixture, along with the lemon zest, and beat. Stir in the sour cream. (The mixture will be stiff.)

4. Use your hands to press the dough into an 8" greased pan. Arrange the apples or other fruit neatly on top of cake.

5. Grind the almonds in a coffee grinder until fine. Combine the almonds with the remaining ingredients. Mixture will be lumpy (don't over-mix). Sprinkle topping over fruit-covered cake.

6. Bake at 350°F for 30 minutes, or until a cake tester comes out clean. Let cool. Serve in pan.

swirly border

It's very difficult to find purchased pillowcases that are easy to stitch through, because most come in tightly woven, 400-thread-count fabrics. To overcome this challenge, I purchased fabric and stitched up my own. Making them is so simple, you won't want to stop until you have a whole drawer full of them! I chose white linen fabric, but a pretty colored cotton would be just as nice. When you select your fabric, make sure a needle will easily go through it.

FINISHED SIZE: 20" x 30"

FABRIC

1¼ yards of 45" white cotton or linen fabric

THREAD

Two 8.7-yard, 6-strand skeins of cotton embroidery floss

I used DMC 792 (dark blue).

NOTIONS

Size 22 chenille needle

White sewing thread

STITCHES

Chain Stitch
(page 26)

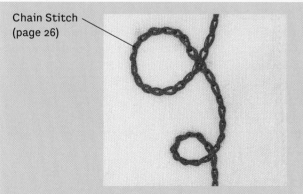

PREPARING THE FABRIC

1. Wash the fabric to remove sizing.
2. Measure and cut a 43" × 37" rectangle from the fabric (see page 44).
3. Referring to the diagram on page 191, use a see-through ruler and a water-soluble or child's washable marker to measure and mark the guidelines.
4. Turn under one of the 43" sides ½". Press. Machine-stitch close to the fold. Bring the two 37" sides together by folding the fabric in half widthwise; pin. Pin along the other unsewn edge. Machine-stitch along both pinned edges, taking a ½" seam. Trim the two corners. Turn the pillowcase to the outside. Press with a hot iron.
5. Use a photocopier to enlarge the Swirly Border pattern on page 191 by 250%. With the centerline of the border matched to the 10½" guideline, use the tracing paper method or a water-soluble or child's washable marker to transfer the design to the fabric. (See page 19.)

STITCHING THE DESIGN

Use three strands of floss throughout, and make sure you are working on the right side of the fabric.

6. Work Chain Stitch along the swirly loops. Make your stitches about ⅛" to ³⁄₁₆" long.

FINISHING THE PILLOWCASE

7. Neaten the thread ends by trimming to ¼", and remove all marking lines. With the embroidered side face down on the ironing board, press, using the steam setting to set the stitches. Spritz more water on the fabric with a spray bottle for additional moisture as you press. Try not to get moisture on the 6" fold line or it will disappear.
8. With your embroidery on the outside, turn under along the 6" guideline; pin. Machine-stitch this hem close to the original stitching. (The wrong side of your embroidery will be hidden within the wide hem.)

it's a mod, mod, flowered world

FINISHED SIZE: 20" x 30"

FABRIC

1¼ yards of 45" cotton or linen fabric

THREAD

One 8.7-yard, 6-strand skein of cotton embroidery floss in *each* of three colors.

I used Anchor 87 (fuchsia), 316 (orange), and 54 (bright coral).

NOTIONS

Size 22 chenille needle

White sewing thread

STITCHES

Blanket Stitch (page 26)

Satin Stitch (page 23)

Stem Stitch (page 25)

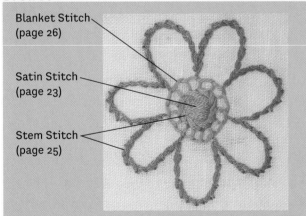

PREPARING THE FABRIC

1. Wash the fabric to remove sizing.
2. Measure and cut a 43" × 37" rectangle from the fabric (see page 44).
3. Referring to the diagram on page 192, use a see-through ruler and a water-soluble or child's washable marker to measure and mark guidelines.
4. Turn under one of the 43" sides ½". Press. Machine-stitch close to the fold. Bring the two 37" sides together by folding fabric in half widthwise; pin. Pin along other unsewn edge. Machine-stitch along both pinned edges, taking a ½" seam. Trim the two corners. Turn pillowcase to outside. Press with a hot iron.
5. Use a photocopier to enlarge the It's a Mod, Mod, Flowered World pattern on page 192 by 167%. Place the center of the flower on one of the five marks you made in step 3, and use the tracing paper method or a water-soluble or child's washable marker to transfer the flower motif to the fabric (see page 19). Repeat this step for each of other four marks on the line.

STITCHING THE DESIGN

Use three strands of floss for stitching all the designs.

6. **For flowers 1, 3, and 5.** Using coral, work the center of each flower in Satin Stitch; outline the center with Stem Stitch. Using orange, work Blanket Stitch around the flower center, carrying the legs of the stitch toward the center. Using fuchsia, outline each petal in Stem Stitch.
7. **For flowers 2 and 4.** Using orange, work the center of each flower in Satin Stitch; outline the center with Stem Stitch. Using fuchsia, work Blanket Stitch around the flower center, carrying the legs of the stitch toward the center. Using coral, outline each petal in Stem Stitch.

FINISHING THE PILLOWCASE

Follow the finishing instructions for Swirly Border, page 131.

please stitch the daisies

FINISHED SIZE: 21" x 30"

GROUND FABRIC

1¼ yards of 45"-wide cotton or linen fabric for each pillowcase

THREAD

One 8.7-yard, 6-strand skein of cotton embroidery floss in *each* of three colors.

I used Anchor 312 (yellow), 29 (red), and 256 (green).

NOTIONS

Size 22 chenille needle

White sewing thread

STITCHES

Lazy Daisy Stitch (page 27)

Satin Stitch (page 23)

Stem Stitch (page 25)

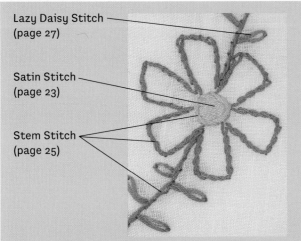

PREPARING THE FABRIC

1. Wash the fabric to remove sizing.
2. Measure and cut a 43" × 37" rectangle from the fabric (see page 44.)
3. Referring to the diagram on page 193, use a see-through ruler and a water-soluble or child's washable marker to measure and mark guidelines.
4. Turn under one of the 43" sides ½". Press. Machine-stitch close to the fold. Bring the two 37" sides together by folding the fabric in half widthwise; pin. Pin along the other unsewn edge. Machine-stitch along both pinned edges. Trim the two corners. Turn pillowcase to the outside. Press with a hot iron.
5. Use a photocopier to enlarge the Please Stitch the Daisies pattern on page 193 by 250%. With the highest point of the design matched to the stitching guideline, use the tracing paper method or a water-soluble or child's washable marker to transfer the design to the fabric. (See page 19.)

STITCHING THE DESIGN

Use three strands of floss for stitching all the designs.

6. Using yellow, work the center of each flower in Satin Stitch; outline the centers with Stem Stitch.
7. Using red, outline each petal in Stem Stitch. If the Stem Stitches fall down at the curves, use anchoring stitches to keep them in place. (See illustration on page 25.)
8. Using green, work the trailing vine in Stem Stitch.
9. Using green, work leaves in Lazy Daisy Stitch, randomly spaced on both sides of the stem. Make six to eight leaves per stem section.

FINISHING THE PILLOWCASE

Follow the instructions for Swirly Border, page 131.

It's a Crewel World

I've always loved doing crewelwork. My first experience was in the 1970s. My four sisters and I each worked a small crewelwork kit that depicted a different vegetable. My mom framed our completed stitcheries for her wall, where they hung for many years. I spent hundreds of happy hours with other projects, learning different stitches while creating pictures of little girls and animals that were popular at that time.

Crewelwork is a form of embroidery that uses wool yarn on cotton or linen ground fabrics. It was extremely popular in American Colonial days when needleworkers used it to depict fanciful floral designs on handwoven fabrics that were then sewn into bed coverings and curtains. During the Colonial Revival of the 1950s, crewelwork experienced a revival of its own, thanks in part to wonderful collections at museums like those at Historic Deerfield (Deerfield, Massachusetts) and Colonial Williamsburg (Williamsburg, Virginia).

golden sea of wildflowers

For this spirited trio of crewelwork pillows, I chose bright-colored linens for the ground fabrics. The bold colors of beautiful wool yarns on the bright grounds make this an exuberant threesome with a retro-hippy look. They strike a balance between traditional crewelwork and its use in modern homes. With their large number of stitches, these designs are great vehicles for increasing your stitchery skills. An embroidery hoop is useful for this technique.

FINISHED SIZE: 14" x 14"

FABRICS

½ yard of bright yellow, suit-weight linen, for front

½ yard contrasting-color cotton fabric, for pillow back

THREAD

One 8-yard, 3-ply skein *each* of Persian wool in nine colors.

I used Paternayan, Christmas Green/697, Coffee Brown/420, Hot Pink/961, Periwinkle/341, Strawberry/953, Caribbean Blue/592, Lavender/331, Spice/850, and Salmon/843.

NOTIONS

Size 20 chenille needle

Embroidery hoop

14" pillow insert (preferably down)

STITCHES

A Blanket Stitch (page 26)

B Chain Stitch (page 26)

C Feather Stitch (page 28)

D Fly Stitch (page 27)

E French Knot (page 29)

F Laid Stitch (page 30)

PREPARING THE FABRIC

1. Measure and cut a 17" square from the linen for the pillow front (see page 44.)
2. Measure and cut the pillow back fabric for either a non-removable cover or a flapped back opening for a 14" square pillow (see page 48.) Set pillow back aside.
3. Use a photocopier to increase the Golden Sea of Wildflowers pattern on page 194 by 400%. Making sure the design is centered, transfer the design to the fabric using the tracing paper or light table method (see page 19). You will have 1½" extra fabric around all sides of the design so that you can use an embroidery hoop.

STITCHING THE DESIGN

Use an embroidery hoop, moving it around as you stitch each individual motif. (See To Hoop or Not to Hoop, page 45.) Unless otherwise noted, work all stitches with a single strand of Persian wool.

4. **Lower left flower:**
   - Using dark brown, outline the two center rings and flower stem in Stem Stitch.
   - Using bright green, fill the stem with Stem Stitch, packed tightly together.
   - Using hot pink, work Blanket Stitch around outer center ring.
   - Using periwinkle, work the center ring in French Knots, packed tightly together; work each of the six vertical rays in Feather Stitch; and work the terminal "scoop" of each ray in Stem Stitch.

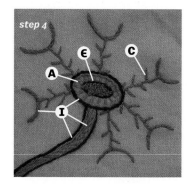

step 4

G Satin Stitch (page 23)

H Spider Web Stitch (page 31)

I Stem Stitch (page 25)

J Straight Stitch (page 24)

K Needleweaving Stitch (page 31)

5. Middle flower:

- Using dark brown, outline all shapes except the three inner circles and the five small petals with Stem Stitch.
- Using bright green, fill the stem and leaves with Stem Stitch, packed tightly together.
- Using orange, fill the two outer sections of the flower with Stem Stitch, packed tightly together.
- Using two strands of coral, work the top horizontal section of the flower in Satin Stitch.
- Using periwinkle, work the three central circles in Spider Web Stitch, and work the top five flower petals in Needleweaving.

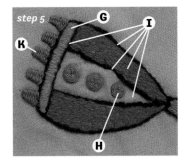

6. Middle right flower:

- Using dark brown, outline the center with Stem Stitch.
- Using turquoise, fill the center with Chain Stitch, packed tightly together, beginning at the outside and working toward the center. (See page 61.)

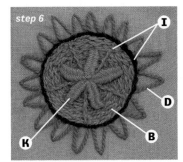

- Using hot pink, work the five rays in Stem Stitch over the turquoise-filled center.
- Using coral, work five bars of Needleweaving to create the flower center between each of the hot pink rays (refer to photo).
- Using violet, work Fly Stitch around the outside of the circle; for greater interest, make the petals different sizes.

7. Upper left flower:

- Using dark brown, outline the entire flower, flower center, and leaves in Stem Stitch.
- Using two strands of turquoise for one half and bright green for the other, fill the leaves with Satin Stitch.
- Using salmon, fill the flower center with Chain Stitch, packed tightly together.

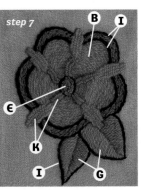

- Using periwinkle, fill the outer rim of the flower with Stem Stitch, packed tightly together, and fill the flower center with French Knots, packed tightly together.
- Using bright green, work five small bars of Needleweaving, radiating from the flower center; match these bars up with the indentations on the outer rim of the flower.
- Using hot pink, work five leaf-shaped Needleweaving bars at the ends of the bright green Needleweaving bars, protruding ¼" from the flower rim.

8. Upper right flower:

- Using dark brown, outline the center and outer edges of the flower and stem in Stem Stitch.
- Using bright green, fill the stem with Stem Stitch, packed tightly together, and work the leaves in Needleweaving.

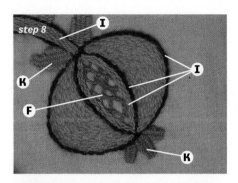

step 8

- Using hot pink, fill the outer sections of the flower with Chain Stitch, packed tightly together.
- Using turquoise, work three closely packed rows of Stem Stitch to outline the flower center.
- Using violet, work diagonal lines of Laid Stitch in the flower center, and work the three upper leaves in Needleweaving.

9. **Lower right stem:**
   - Using dark brown, outline the stem edges in Stem Stitch.
   - Using bright green, fill the stem with Stem Stitch, packed closely together, and work the leaves in Needleweaving.

10. **Small flower in upper middle:**
    - Using dark brown, outline the flower center in Stem Stitch.
    - Using periwinkle, fill flower center with closely packed Chain Stitch, beginning at the outside and working toward the center.
    - Using orange, work three lines of Stem Stitch, radiating from the center of flower on top of the periwinkle.
    - Using hot pink, work a bar in Needleweaving between each of the brick red rays.
    - With turquoise, work Fly Stitch around edge of circle for petals; for greater interest, vary the sizes.

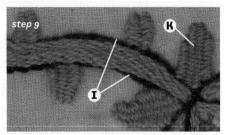

step 9

FINISHING THE PILLOW

11. Neaten the thread ends by trimming to ¼", and remove all marking lines. Block and press the pillow front from the wrong side, with the embroidery face down on a terry cloth towel (see page 21). Take care not to squish the stitching too much. Trim the ends to ¼".
12. Keeping the design centered, trim the pillow front to 15" × 15".
13. With right sides facing, stitch the front and back together, taking a ½" seam and following the instructions on pages 48–49 for the type of backing you chose.
14. Stuff with pillow insert.

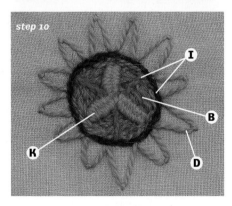

step 10

four-petaled flower

FINISHED SIZE: 12" x 12"

FABRICS

½ yard turquoise suit-weight linen, for pillow front

½ yard cotton fabric, for pillow back

THREAD

One 8-yard, 3-ply skein *each* of Persian wool in yellow, dark brown, hot pink, turquoise, bright green, and orange

I used Paternayan, Autumn Yellow/724, Coffee Brown/420, Hot Pink/961, Caribbean Blue/592, Christmas Green/697, and Spice/853.

NOTIONS

Size 20 chenille needle

Embroidery hoop

12" pillow insert (preferably down)

STITCHES

A Chain Stitch (page 26)

B Stem Stitch (page 25)

C Needleweaving (page 31)

D French Knot (page 29)

E Laid Stitch (page 30)

F Cross Stitch (page 24)

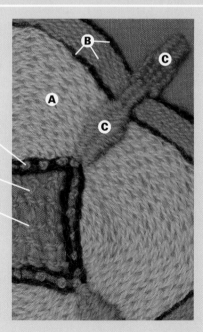

PREPARING THE FABRIC

1. Measure and cut a 15" square from the linen for the pillow front (see page 44).
2. Measure and cut the pillow back fabric for either a non-removable cover or a flapped back opening for a 12" square pillow (see page 48). Set pillow back aside.
3. Use a photocopier to enlarge the Four-Petaled Flower pattern on page 192 by 250%. Using the tracing paper or light table method, transfer the design to the fabric, taking care to center the design.

STITCHING THE DESIGN

Use an embroidery hoop, moving it around as necessary. (See To Hoop or Not to Hoop, page 45.) Unless otherwise noted, work all stitches with a single strand of Persian wool.

4. Using dark brown, outline the inner and outer rims of the flower center and the petals with Stem Stitch.
5. Using hot pink, fill the outer rim of the petals with Stem Stitch, packed tightly together.
6. Using yellow, fill the petals with Chain Stitch, packed tightly together.
7. Using orange, work the flower center in Laid Stitch. At each intersection of the Laid Stitch, work a Cross Stitch in hot pink.
8. Using hot pink, fill the space between the two squares with French Knots.
9. Using two strands of turquoise, work a bar in Needleweaving beginning at each corner of the flower center and ending at an inside flower petal.
10. Using two strands of bright green, work a 1¼" leaf in Needleweaving beginning at the end of each of the bars made in step 9 and protruding about ¾" from the flower edge.

FINISHING THE PILLOW

11. Follow the finishing instructions for Golden Sea of Wildflowers (page 138), except trim the pillow front to 13" × 13".

striped vase with flowers

FINISHED SIZE: 12" x 18"

FABRICS

½ yard chartreuse suit-weight linen, for pillow front

½ yard cotton fabric, for pillow back

THREAD

One 8-yard, 3-ply skein *each* of Persian wool in seven colors.

I used Paternayan, Periwinkle/341, Coffee Brown/420, Caribbean Blue/592, Hot Pink/961, Salmon/843, Violet/301, and Christmas Green/697.

NOTIONS

Size 20 chenille needle

Embroidery hoop

12" x 18" pillow insert
(preferably down)

STITCHES

A Blanket Stitch (page 26)

B Chain Stitch (page 26)

C Fly Stitch (page 27)

D French Knot (page 29)

E Lazy Daisy Stitch (page 27)

F Satin Stitch (page 23)

G Stem Stitch (page 25)

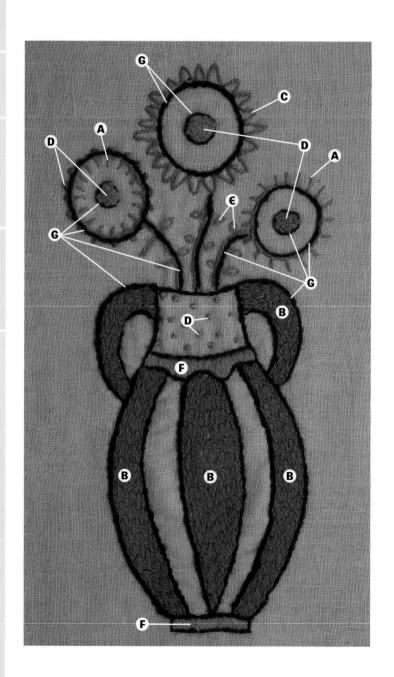

1. Measure and cut a 15" × 21" rectangle from the linen for the pillow front (see page 44).
2. Measure and cut the pillow back fabric for either a non-removable cover or a flapped back opening for a 12" × 18" pillow (see page 48). Set pillow back aside.
3. Use a photocopier to enlarge the Striped Vase with Flowers pattern on page 194 by 333%. Using the tracing paper or light table method, transfer the design to the fabric, taking care to center it (see page 19).

STITCHING THE PILLOW

Use an embroidery hoop, moving it around as necessary. (See To Hoop or Not to Hoop, page 45.) Unless otherwise noted, work all stitches with a single strand of Persian wool.

4. Using dark brown, outline the vase, flower edges, and flower centers in Stem Stitch.
5. **Vase:**
   - Using periwinkle, fill center and two outer stripes of vase and handles with tightly packed Chain Stitch.
   - Using two strands of turquoise, work bottom and vase collar in Satin Stitch; work randomly spaced French Knots in vase top.
6. **Flower stems:**
   - Using bright green, outline the stems in Stem Stitch; work four or five randomly spaced leaves in Lazy Daisy Stitch on each stem.
   - Using dark brown, fill the stems with Stem Stitch.
7. **Left Flower:**
   - Using salmon, outline edge of flower in Blanket Stitch, with legs about ¼" long and pointing toward center of flower.
   - Using violet, work French Knots around outer edge of flower.
   - With hot pink, fill flower center with French Knots, packed tightly together.

8. **Center Flower:**
   - Using violet, form rays around outer edge of flower with Fly Stitch, varying length of stitches.
   - Using salmon, fill center with tightly packed French Knots.
9. **Right Flower:**
   - Using hot pink, work Blanket Stitch around the outer edge of the flower, making the legs about ¼" long and facing away from the flower center.
   - Using violet, fill center with tightly packed French Knots.

FINISHING THE PILLOW

10. Neaten thread ends by trimming to ¼"; remove all marking lines. Block and press pillow front from wrong side, with embroidery face down on a terry cloth towel (see page 21). Trim ends to ¼".
11. Keeping design centered, trim pillow front to 13" × 19".
12. With right sides facing, stitch the front and back together, taking a ½" seam and following the instructions on pages 48–49 for the type of backing you chose.
13. Stuff with pillow insert.

A Timeless Fabric

Crewelwork is an entire industry unto itself in India. Bolts of off-white, coarsely woven cotton are decorated with free-flowing florals in many different colors of wool. These fabrics are embraced by upscale decorators for upholstered sofas and wing chairs. Crewelwork fabrics have an enduring quality to them, working equally well in contemporary and historic interiors.

Blowin' in the Wind!

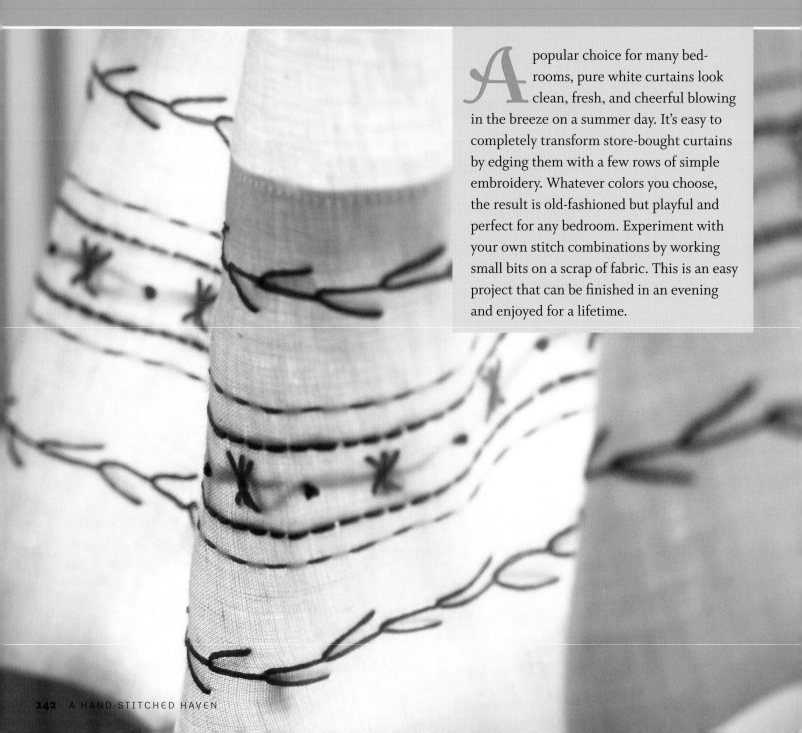

A popular choice for many bedrooms, pure white curtains look clean, fresh, and cheerful blowing in the breeze on a summer day. It's easy to completely transform store-bought curtains by edging them with a few rows of simple embroidery. Whatever colors you choose, the result is old-fashioned but playful and perfect for any bedroom. Experiment with your own stitch combinations by working small bits on a scrap of fabric. This is an easy project that can be finished in an evening and enjoyed for a lifetime.

I chose my favorite bright colors of hot pink, orange, and green, but the curtains would look equally nice in a combination of earth tones or of chalky pastel shades. Or, for a subtle but elegant look, work the embroidery in white for a whispering tone-on-tone effect.

FABRIC

Purchased cotton or linen curtains

THREAD

Three 8.7-yard, 6-strand skeins of cotton embroidery floss and two skeins *each* of two other colors.

I used three skeins of Anchor 63 (hot pink) and two skeins each of Anchor 925 (orange) and 257 (green).

NOTIONS

Size 20 chenille needle

STITCHES

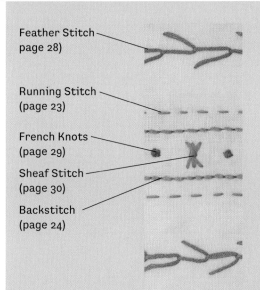

Feather Stitch
page 28)

Running Stitch
(page 23)

French Knots
(page 29)

Sheaf Stitch
(page 30)

Backstitch
(page 24)

PREPARING THE FABRIC

1. Wash the curtains to remove sizing; press.
2. Using a gridded see-through ruler and a water-soluble or child's washable marker, measure up from the bottom of the curtain and draw six guidelines at 2", 3", 3¼", 4¼", 4½", and 5½". Between the center two lines, mark a dot every ⅝", centered between the lines. (See page 195 for diagram.)

STITCHING THE DESIGN

3. Using six strands of embroidery floss, work the following stitches along the guidelines, starting with the bottom line:
   - Feather Stitch in hot pink
   - Running Stitch in orange
   - Backstitch in green
   - Backstitch in green
   - Running Stitch in orange
   - Feather Stitch in hot pink
4. Using hot pink, work French Knots at every other dot between the two lines of green Backstitch.
5. Using orange, work Sheaf Stitch at the alternate dots between the green lines.

FINISHING THE CURTAINS

6. Neaten the thread ends by trimming to ¼", and remove all marking lines. With the curtain facing down, using a steam setting, iron the back side of the curtain to set the stitches; spritz with additional water as needed.

Blanketed with Love

The birth of a baby is one of the most special times in a family's life. Babies deserve to be welcomed into the world with lovely things, and for me, lovely things are those made with love by the hands of a friend. Warm and snuggly for both baby and parent, a hand-embroidered baby blanket covers all the bases. These soft textures and beautiful colors are cuddly and nurturing. I pre-washed this lovely vintage piece of pure wool in the washing machine to felt it slightly. Washing made it softer and fluffier, and it also pre-shrunk the wool, so that it can now be machine-washed on gentle. When you're giving the blanket as a present, tuck a little tag in the gift box that says "Gentle machine-wash in cold water." If the blanket shrinks a little more, it's okay. I used one ball of worsted-weight wool knitting yarn for all the stitchery. If you're a knitter, this is a great way to use up your stash.

FINISHED SIZE: 36" x 36"

FABRIC

1¼ yards light- to medium-weight wool fabric, pre-washed in hot water with a cold rinse

THREAD

One skein worsted-weight wool knitting yarn.

I used Nashua Handknits Julia (50% wool/25% alpaca/25% mohair), 93 yd (85 m)/1.75 oz (50 gm) skeins in Zinnia Pink/5084.

NOTIONS

Size 18 chenille needle

STITCHES

Backstitch (page 24)

Blanket Stitch (page 26)

Chain Stitch (page 26)

French Knot (page 29)

babes in the wool

I'm always asked, why wool? and, aren't you afraid of allergies? My theory is that if you start babies out with wool, they won't be allergic to it. You can't beat it for warmth and washability. What if the baby throws up on it? Wash it. The sheep that donated their fiber to that baby's blanket were outside in the elements and wool washes great. Still not convinced? Then work this project on polyester fleece — it will still be cute and cuddly.

PREPARING THE FABRIC

1. Measure and cut a 36" square from the wool (see page 44).
2. Use a photocopier to increase the Blanketed with Love pattern on page 192 by 250%. Using your very best handwriting, write out the baby's name and birth date, centered within the heart. If you don't feel confident about your handwriting, use your computer to design the type, following the instructions on page 68.
3. Transfer the design to a corner of your fabric using the tracing paper method (see page 19). The bottom point of the heart should be 5" from the corner. Using a water-soluble or child's washable marker, draw over the traced lines to make the stitching lines clear.

STITCHING THE DESIGN

4. Work the name in Backstitch. For separate letters, end each one with a stitched knot before beginning the next letter. Dot the letters *i* and *j* with French Knots.
5. Work the date in Backstitch, and use French Knots for the dashes in the date.
6. Outline the heart in Chain Stitch.
7. Work Blanket Stitch around the entire edge. You will need to start and end the yarn frequently, as Blanket Stitch uses a lot of yarn. Start with a knot on the wrong side, and when the yarn is almost finished, take several small stitches on the wrong side into one of the legs of the closest stitch to end off the piece. Leave the tails long until after washing the blanket. Turn the corners by working three stitches, as shown on page 26.

FINISHING THE BLANKET

8. Machine-wash the blanket on gentle cycle in cold water to set the stitches. Press with a steam iron when dry.
9. Trim any yarn ends.

Julia's teddy bears are made of felted wool from sweaters and blankets dyed in fun colors. I made two, and my Mom, my 12-year-old niece Olivia, and my friend Gwen each made one. It's fun to have several friends use the same bear pattern, as each person's hands craft a different body shape and different facial expressions. Teddy bears can be grumpy or happy, chubby or skinny, serene or perplexed.

I like to stuff my bears with either wool or cotton, which gives them more heft compared to those stuffed with polyester fiberfill. You can use yarn or fabric scraps cut into small pieces to fit easily into the recesses of the legs and arms.

FINISHED SIZE: 11" long

FABRIC

Small pieces of wool blankets or wool sweaters, felted and dyed fun colors (cashmere or angora are especially soft) or 9" x 12" squares of purchased wool felt in three different colors for each bear

- For the body and ears, two pieces of the same color approximately 13" long and 10" wide
- For the belly and nose, a 3" square for each

THREAD

One 8-yard, 3-ply skein of Persian wool

I used Paternayan, Coffee Brown/420.

NOTIONS

Size 20 chenille needle

Wool or cotton yarn or fabric scraps, for stuffing

STITCHES

A Blanket Stitch (page 26)

B Satin Stitch (page 23)

C Straight Stitch (page 22)

PREPARING THE FABRIC

1. Using a photocopier, enlarge the four pattern pieces for the Teddy Bear on page 195 by 250%. (The body pattern will fit perfectly on a standard letter-size sheet, 8½ × 11".) Cut the pattern pieces out.
2. Lay body pattern (D) on felt fabric, and trace around pattern with a water-soluble or child's washable marker. Cut two pieces exactly alike. Trace and cut two ears (A) from same fabric.
3. Trace and cut one nose (B) from another color of felt.
4. Trace and cut one tummy (C) from a third color of felt.

STITCHING THE DESIGN

See page 26, and Tricks with Layers, page 158, for advice on sewing felted pieces together with stitchery.

5. **Ears.** Using one strand of wool, work Blanket Stitch around the rounded portion of each ear.
6. **Nose.** Pin the nose to one of the body pieces. Using one strand of wool, attach nose to body by working Blanket Stitch around edge of nose, stitching through both layers of fabric.
7. **Belly.** Pin belly to same body piece. Attach as for nose.
8. **Eyes.** Using a water-soluble or child's washable marker, mark a circle for each eye, as shown on pattern. Using two strands of wool, work eye in Satin Stitch. After you've made one layer, work more Satin Stitch on top of the first to create dimension. You can even out the shape on the second or third pass.
9. **Nose.** Using a water-soluble or child's washable marker, draw a triangle for the nose, as shown on pattern. Using two strands of wool, work nose in Satin Stitch. Add another layer of stitches on top of the first, as you did for the eyes.
10. **Mouth.** Using two strands of wool, work two Straight Stitches below the nose to make a mouth, as shown on the pattern.
11. **Body.** With wrong sides facing, pin front and back body pieces together. Beginning at the right side where the neck and arms join, work Blanket Stitch all the way around the body in this order: first arm, both legs, and, finally, second arm.
12. **Ears.** When you reach head section, position ears as shown on pattern, sandwiching them between front and back layers, and extending them about ¼" into the body. Continue stitch-

ing around head, working Blanket Stitch in two steps at the ears (see Blanket Stitch, Interrupted, page 117).

13. Continue around head, treating second ear in the same manner as the first. When you are 2" from where you began, park the threaded needle in the fabric.

14. Stuff the bear with your chosen stuffing material, using the unsharpened end of a pencil to poke the stuffing all the way to the ends of the arms and legs. When the bear is sufficiently fat (or thin — you decide, as you are birthing it!), complete the Blanket Stitch edging to close the stuffing in the body.

FINISHING THE BEAR

15. Using a steam iron, steam the bear to even out the stitching, taking care not to squish the bear.

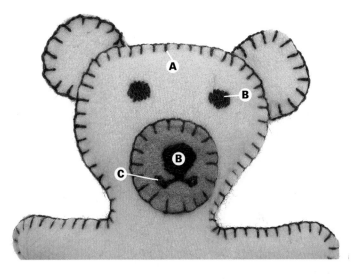

In the Lap of Luxury

I've always loved the classic paisley motif. Exotic and organic, it lends itself well to all kinds of needlework and design. In our traveling days, Mark and I ventured to the Paisley Shawl Museum in Paisley, Scotland, to satisfy my fascination. We even named our first border collie Paisley.

I decided to pay homage to the paisley shawl by recreating the motif with a contemporary feel on this purchased cashmere throw. A wool throw would work just as well. My updated rendition is completely different from those historic samples found at museums. My stitches are bigger and looser. My own modern heirloom gives a new aesthetic identity to the antique motif.

FINISHED SIZE: 52" x 72"

FABRIC

Purchased pumpkin-colored cashmere or wool throw with fringe

THREAD

Three 8-yard, 3-ply skeins *each* of Persian wool in turquoise and green; two skeins in navy blue; and one skein in fuchsia.

I used Paternayan, three skeins each of Caribbean Blue/591 and Loden Green/692; two skeins of Navy Blue/571; and one skein of Fuchsia/351.

NOTIONS

Size 20 chenille needle

STITCHES

A French Knot (page 29)

B Lazy Daisy Stitch (page 27)

C Running Stitch (page 23)

D Stem Stitch (page 25)

E Straight Stitch (page 24)

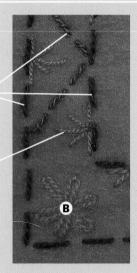

PREPARING THE FABRIC

1. Using a gridded see-through ruler and a water-soluble or child's washable marker, draw a line 6" from the edge at both fringed ends, beginning and ending 1" from sides. Draw a line 1" from each side. Draw a second rectangle 1" inside the larger rectangle to create the border. (See diagram on page 196.)

2. Using a water-soluble or child's washable marker and beginning 2" from the corner of outer border line, draw a cross line every 2¼" between the two border lines. As you near the next corner, you may need to adjust the distance between the lines. These are the reference points for the zigzag stitching.

3. Use a photocopier to increase the Fringed Paisley Throw pattern on page 196 by 333%. Make one copy exactly like the template and a second copy the reverse image of it. Use the tracing paper method to transfer a paisley motif to each corner of the throw. Direct the point of the paisley toward the center of throw, and position outer edge of paisley 1" from inner guideline, using whichever version of the template you need to orient the paisley as shown in diagram. Retrace the lines with water-soluble or child's washable marker.

STITCHING THE DESIGN

Use one strand of Persian wool throughout.

4. **Border:**
   - Using navy blue, work Running Stitch along both border lines. On the right side, these stitches should be about ½" long, and on the wrong side, they should be about ⅛" long.
   - Using fuchsia, work one Lazy Daisy Stitch in each corner between the border lines.
   - Using turquoise, work three Running Stitches diagonally connecting two of the cross lines marked in step 2. Make these stitches from one side of the border to the other, zigzag fashion, around the throw.
   - Using green, work a half star with five points in Straight Stitch, placing the center point of the star on the border line in the space within the zigzag motif.

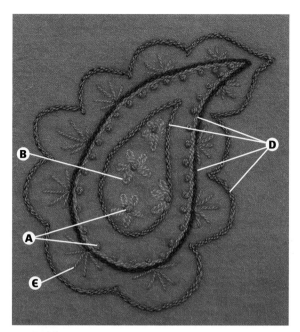

5. Paisley:
- Using turquoise, work the curved border in Stem Stitch.
- Using navy blue, work the outer pear shape in Stem Stitch.
- Using fuchsia, work another line of Stem Stitch just inside the navy blue stitching.
- Using turquoise, work the inner pear shape in Stem Stitch.
- Using green, work a line of French Knots just inside the fuchsia Stem Stitch on the outer pear shape; space the knots ¼"–½" apart.
- Using fuchsia, work three or four five-pointed lazy daisies within the inner pear shape.
- Using green, and French Knots, work a knot in the center of each lazy daisy.
- Using green, work a five-pointed half star in Straight Stitch, placing the center point of the star on the navy blue outline of the outer pear, placing one star in each scallop.

FINISHING THE THROW

6. Wash the throw to set the stitches and remove the guidelines. Trim the ends neatly. Using a steam iron, press the throw on the wrong side to avoid flattening the embroidery.

a touch of india

The paisley motif has its roots in the Orient. It is said that a *paisley* (or *boteh*, as it is known in India) looks like a pear or a teardrop. To me, the intriguing shape conjures up thoughts of faraway Eastern bazaars full of hand-embroidered textiles and hand-knotted rugs. Authentic paisley shawls, known in antiquing circles as *kashmir shawls,* combined the paisley motif with wandering vines and flowers in glorious colors.

In the late 1700s, hand-woven or embroidered shawls (there were both kinds) from India were high fashion. The shawls were so expensive that only the richest of the rich could afford them. Ambitious European weavers in France and Britain developed their own machine-woven jacquard technology to imitate the handmade Indian shawls, so they could be sold at a lesser cost.

The name *paisley* comes from the small town of Paisley, Scotland, where professional weavers began producing machine-woven shawls in 1808. Now you'll find these wool shawls at antique stores selling for hundreds of dollars. Modern hand-embroidered Indian shawls are sometimes available, although they are quite hard to come by. If you're going to Scotland, don't miss the Paisley Shawl Museum (High Street, Paisley PA1 2BA; Tel: 0141 889 3151; Fax: 0141 889 9240; e-mail: museums.els@renfrewshire.gov.uk).

Wedding Blanket

When we were first married about 20 years ago, we received a framed embroidery with the message, "Mark + Kristin" and the date of our marriage. It was stitched by a good friend with whom I'd gone to textile school. I wasn't so sure about the gift, and I didn't particularly want to get married then (I was — and am — a feminist!), but I'd found the most wonderful man in the world. To appease my mom, we got married. We're still happily married, and marriage didn't get in the way of my quite interesting career in yarns and needlework. And we still have that little embroidery in our bedroom. It has grown on me, just as the years have. I think about all the wonderful and difficult things that Mark and I have experienced as time has passed. I think about all the gifts people stitch for friends, and it makes me happy that I can pass on some of these ideas for others to use as gifts for *their* special friends.

wedding blanket

A great wedding or anniversary present, a good wool blanket will envelop a couple in warmth and love for years. I positioned the stitchery so it shows when a bed sheet is folded over the edge. You could make a smaller version for a framed picture.

FINISHED SIZE: Your choice

FABRIC

Purchased wool blanket with Whip Stitch edging

THREAD

One 8-yard, 3-ply skein *each* of Persian wool in dark brown, turquoise, bright green, bittersweet, violet, and periwinkle

I used Paternayan, Coffee Brown/420, Caribbean Blue/592, Christmas Green/697, Bittersweet/832, Violet/301, and Periwinkle/341.

NOTIONS

Size 20 chenille needle

STITCHES

Blanket Stitch (page 26)

French Knots (page 29)

Stem Stitch (page 25)

Straight Stitch (page 24)

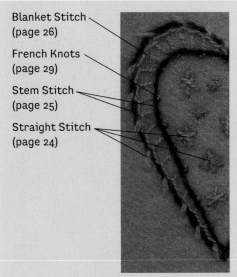

PREPARING THE BLANKET

1. Write the text on a piece of paper. Names should be about 2½" tall and date about 1½" tall, centered beneath the names.
2. With a photocopier increase the Wedding Blanket pattern (page 196) by 200%.
3. Measure and mark the center of the blanket at the top edge, then follow the guidelines on the diagram on page 196 for placement of the hearts and lettering. Use the tracing paper method (see page 19) to transfer the motifs to the blanket. Using a water-soluble or child's washable marker, draw over the traced lines to make the letters easier to see.

STITCHING THE DESIGN

Use one strand of Persian wool throughout except where noted.

4. **Lettering:**
   - Using periwinkle, work Stem Stitch along all of the lettering. For spaced letters, tie off the yarn on the back side by making a stitched knot. Work the dots and punctuation with French Knots.
5. **Hearts:**
   - Using dark brown, outline the inner and outer hearts on each heart motif in Stem Stitch.
   - Using violet, work Blanket Stitch in the space between the two hearts. Vary the length of the legs to fit into the space as it narrows toward the bottom.
   - Using two strands of bittersweet, work Straight Stitches on top of outer heart outline. Starting at the inside of the line, slant each stitch away from the center from bottom to top.
   - Using bright green, work a line of French Knots just inside the inner heart, spacing the stitches ½" apart.
   - Using both turquoise and periwinkle, fill center of heart with various-sized Straight Stitch stars, randomly spaced; make four or five of each color in the center of each heart.

FINISHING THE BLANKET

6. Wash or dry-clean the blanket to set the stitches and remove the marker lines. Trim the ends neatly.

heart-to-heart pillow

From grade school on, we've used hearts on letters and valentines to express our love and affection for someone dear. Taking handmade hearts to a whole new level, you can hand-stitch a heart decorated with your names or the shorthand for hugs and kisses — XOX. Back the pillow front with bright contrasting fabric, and fill it with soft stuffing along with a little dried lavender, the traditional herb of "remembrance," so you won't be forgotten.

FINISHED SIZE: 11" tall x 11" wide

FABRIC

Two small scraps of felted wool (about ⅓ yard each of two colors of wool), washed and felted

THREAD

One skein worsted-weight wool knitting yarn.

I used Nashua Handknits Julia (50% wool/25% alpaca/ 25% mohair), 93 yd (85 m)/1.75 oz (50 gm) skeins in Magenta/2983.

NOTIONS

Size 18 chenille needle

Small amount of wool, cotton, or polyester fill, for stuffing

Small amount of dried lavender (optional)

STITCHES

Backstitch (page 24)

Blanket Stitch (page 26)

PREPARING THE FABRIC

1. Pre-wash your wool fabric in hot water with a cold rinse if you aren't using felted wool.
2. Use a photocopier to increase the Heart-to-Heart Pillow pattern on page 194 by 500%. Cut out the heart shape and trace it onto both pieces of wool. Cut two hearts.
3. Using the tracing paper method, transfer the XOX to one of the hearts. Use a water-soluble or child's washable marker to trace over letters. Repeat this step on the second heart.

STITCHING THE DESIGN

4. Work the lettering on both heart-shaped pieces in Backstitch.
5. Pin the two pieces together, wrong sides facing. Beginning at the side of the heart about 2" from the point, sandwich the knot between the two layers (see page 158) and stitch toward the point in Blanket Stitch. When you need to start new yarn, sandwich the knot between the layers. End the yarn by making three small stitches between the layers on one of the inside threads of the Blanket Stitch. Stitch all the way around until you get to within 3" of where you began; park your threaded needle on the face of the pillow.

FINISHING THE PILLOW

6. Neaten the thread ends by trimming to ¼", and remove all marking lines. Block the heart by steaming (see page 21).
7. Fill the heart pillow with stuffing, adding some dried lavender, if desired. Using the attached needle and thread, close the opening by completing the line of Blanket Stitch.

His-and-Hers Hot-Water Bottle Cozies

Hot-water bottles are so old-fashioned that they are now trendy. My grandmother definitely knew something: Hot-water heat warms aching muscles and chilly toes. If you're feeling low, a hot-water bottle along with a cup of hot tea will restore your soul. Even cats and dogs love hot-water bottles! Make your pet its very own hot-water bottle cover to snuggle on for a long winter's nap.

I like to hand-stitch a his-and-her pair for an unforgettable shower or wedding present. My version uses a recycled wool blanket, but for the ultimate hot-water bottle cover, look for some cashmere sweaters at thrift shops, felt them, and then turn them into the greatest cozies toes will ever curl up to.

his-and-hers cozies

FINISHED SIZE: 10½" x 17" (or adjusted to fit your hot-water bottle)

FABRIC

¾ yard heavy wool or coating material

THREAD

One skein worsted-weight wool knitting yarn.

I used bits from my stash.

NOTIONS

Size 18 chenille needle

Purchased hot-water bottles

STITCHES

A Blanket Stitch (page 26)

B Lazy Daisy Stitch (page 27)

C Stem Stitch (page 25)

D Straight Stitch (page 24)

tricks with layers

Here's a trick when you're stitching together two or more fabric layers: Pin layers together. Go in through top layer only from wrong side, enclosing knot between layers, then stitch design through both layers. To end, pull threaded needle to inside between layers. Take two or three small stitches on either back sides of stitches or fabric itself. Trim ends and poke thread tail toward middle to completely enclose it.

PREPARING THE FABRIC

1. Felt the wool fabric (see page 46).
2. Use a paper shopping bag to make your pattern (cut the bag open so it lays flat). Lay the hot-water bottle on the paper and trace all the way around it. Remove the hot-water bottle, and measure and draw a 2" line all the way around the first shape to allow for the larger size of the hot-water bottle when it is filled with water. At the point where the neck flares out, eliminate the curve and draw straight up. Cut a second pattern identical to the first.
3. For a pattern for the back, measure 8" down from the top of one of the paper patterns, draw a straight line from side to side, and cut your pattern into two pieces along this line. Tape a strip of paper 1" wide to the top of the lower section; this will form the overlap.
4. Place each of these three pieces on your fabric, trace around them and then cut them out.
5. Use a photocopier to enlarge the His-and-Hers lettering on page 194 by 200%. Centering the lettering on the front of the cozy (see page 18), use the tracing paper method to transfer the design to the fabric. Draw over the tracing with a water-soluble or child's washable marker to make it easier to see.

STITCHING THE DESIGN

Use a single strand of worsted-weight wool knitting yarn throughout.

6. Work the lettering in Stem Stitch.
7. Work the half-crosses above and below the lettering on the "His" cozy in Lazy Daisy Stitch. Work the radiating motif on the "Hers" cozy in Straight Stitch.
8. Work Blanket Stitch across the straight edges of the two back pieces. Make the stitches about ½" long and ½" apart. (If you need a guideline, use a gridded see-through ruler and a water-soluble or child's washable marker to draw a straight line ½" in from the straight edges, and mark every ½ inch. These marks become points for the needle to enter.)

9. With wrong sides facing, pin the lower back piece to the front piece, matching the edges carefully. Pin the upper part of the back to the front, allowing the top to overlap the bottom. Work Blanket Stitch around the entire edge. Make sure you hide the knot and ends of the yarn on the inside of the cozy (see page 158).

FINISHING THE COZY

10. Neaten the thread ends by trimming to ¼", and remove all marking lines. Block the cozies (see page 21) to set the stitches.

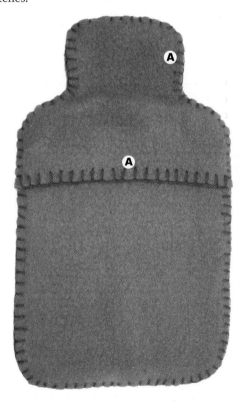

Back of cozy, showing top portion edged with Blanket Stitch and overlapping the bottom

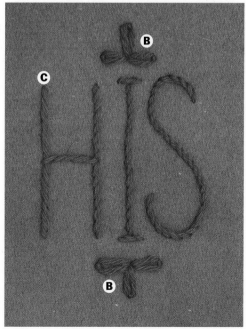

Stitch Yourself Right Out of the Box

I like to think of stitchery as a creative art. And as with any creative art, part of the fun is breaking the rules and using a technique where it isn't expected. Any object can be stitched on, as long as a hole can be made in it and thread can be drawn through it. On the pages that follow, I've stitched on some alternative ground materials, including stationery, boxes, even shoes.

By the time you've worked up some of these not-so-normal stitched projects, your head will be spinning with ideas of what else you can stitch on. What about stitching on wastepaper cans, wooden boxes, lampshades, or notebooks, or using stitchery to decorate the pages of your favorite scrapbook? Think, too, about alternative fibers like ribbons, metal, raffia, or grasses you find outdoors. Let your creative spirit be your guide!

Thinking Outside the Box

These be-ribboned boxes border on the edge of what is considered "real stitchery," but I think it's fun to create colorful objects by combining techniques from different disciplines. Fill these fanciful boxes with floss, Persian wool, and other stitching supplies, or use them for your scrapbooking materials. I used grosgrain ribbon and seam binding tape — from a local sewing store. For a chic-looking container, the secret to success is to combine off-beat colors.

FINISHED SIZE: 8" round

GROUND

A papier-maché box (available at most large craft stores)

THREAD

1 yard *each* of pink seam binding and orange grosgrain ribbon

NOTIONS AND OTHER SUPPLIES

Tapestry needle with an eye large enough to accommodate the ribbon

Paintbrush and periwinkle blue acrylic paint

Polyurethane spray finish (optional)

Awl and hammer

Tape

Glue gun and glue

PREPARING THE BOX

1. Paint both the outside and inside of the box and lid with two coats of the periwinkle blue acrylic paint, allowing the paint to dry between coats. If desired, waterproof the box by spraying it with polyurethane.

2. Using an awl and hammer, and working from the outside in, punch a hole in the exact center of the lid. To prevent the lid from collapsing, support the center with a folded towel or piece of foam.

STITCHING THE DESIGN

3. Before stitching, iron the ribbon to get rid of creases. Thread the needle with 1 yard of the pink seam binding and pull it through the center hole from the inside out, leaving a 1" tail of binding on the inside of the lid. Tape the binding to the lid to secure it.

4. Bring the binding across the top of the lid, over the edge, across the inside of the lid, and back up through the center hole; tug it gently but firmly to tighten it. Tape the binding smoothly against the inside lip of the lid so that the box will close. Repeat this process three more times to form a four-armed cross; taping each piece on the inside as before. When the fourth arm is completed, carry the ribbon to the center on the inside, and cut and tape it where it meets the center. (See diagram on page 197.)

5. Where the binding emerges from the center hole on the top, arrange it so that it puffs nicely.

6. Repeat this process with the orange grosgrain ribbon, making this cross between the arms of the first cross.

FINISHING THE BOX

7. Remove the tape that is holding the tails of binding, and use a glue gun to secure the tails with a tiny dab of glue. On the inside lip of the lid, use a glue gun to secure each section of ribbon so it won't shift. Trim the ends.

six-sided green box

FINISHED SIZE: 7¾"

GROUND

A papier-maché box (available at most large craft stores)

THREAD

1 yard *each* of blue and pink seam bindings and orange grosgrain ribbon

NOTIONS AND OTHER SUPPLIES

Tapestry needle with an eye large enough to accommodate the ribbon

Paintbrush and green acrylic paint

Polyurethane spray finish (optional)

Awl and hammer

Tape

Glue gun and glue

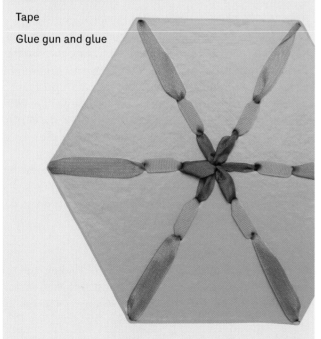

PREPARING THE BOX

1. Paint box and lid, inside and out, with two coats of the green acrylic paint, allowing paint to dry between coats. If desired, waterproof the box by spraying it with polyurethane.
2. With an awl and hammer, working from outside in, punch a hole in exact center of lid (A). (See diagram on page 197.) To prevent lid from collapsing, support center with folded towel or piece of foam.
3. With a pencil and a see-through ruler, lightly mark straight lines from center to each of the six corners. Mark points on each line 1" (B) and 2" (C) from center. Punch a hole at each mark, as in step 2. Punch a hole at each of the six corners, just inside the edge (D). You now have 19 holes.

STITCHING THE DESIGN

4. Before stitching, iron ribbon to get rid of creases. Thread needle with blue seam binding and pull it through center hole (A) from inside out, leaving a 1" tail of binding on inside of lid. Tape binding to lid to secure it.
5. Stitch from center hole (A) down through a hole at B, and back up through A; repeat at each hole B. Arrange ribbon as you stitch so it puffs nicely. After sixth hole, draw ribbon to inside at center, tape end, and trim to 1".
6. Thread needle with orange grosgrain ribbon. Working from inside out, draw needle through a hole at B, leaving a 1" tail on the inside; tape tail. Working toward lid edge on same line, stitch down through a hole at C, and go back up through at hole at B on the adjacent line. Continue in this manner until you have filled the second set of holes with orange ribbon.
7. Repeat step 6 with the pink grosgrain ribbon, stitching from C to D on each of the six lines.

FINISHING THE BOX

8. Using a glue gun or tacky, quick-drying glue, glue the ends of the ribbon on the inside of the lid in place. Let dry.

six-sided pink box

FINISHED SIZE: 8½"

GROUND

A papier-maché box (available at most large craft stores)

THREAD

1 yard *each* of purple, turquoise, and lime-green polka-dot grosgrain ribbon

NOTIONS AND OTHER SUPPLIES

Tapestry needle with an eye large enough to accommodate the ribbon

Paintbrush and light pink acrylic paint

Polyurethane spray finish (optional)

Awl and hammer

Tape

Glue gun and glue

PREPARING THE BOX

1. Paint both outside and inside of box and lid with two coats of pink acrylic paint, allowing paint to dry between coats. If desired, waterproof the box by spraying it with polyurethane.

2. Place your see-through ruler on box lid, aligning ruler edge with opposite corners. Lightly draw a 6" pencil line, centered between the corners. (Line will not go all the way to edge of box.) Do same for each of the other two pairs of corners. The point where the lines intersect is exact center of lid (A). (See diagram on page 198.) Using an awl and hammer, and working from the outside in, punch a hole here. To prevent lid from collapsing, support center with a folded towel or piece of foam.

3. Mark points on each 6" line 1" (B), 2" (C) and 3" (D) from center. Punch a hole at each mark, as in step 2. You now have 19 holes.

STITCHING THE DESIGN

4. Follow same procedure as for green box, using purple from A to B, lime green from B to C, and turquoise from C to D.

FINISHING THE BOX

5. Using a glue gun or tacky, quick-drying glue, glue the ribbon in place on the inside of the lid. Let dry.

Crafty Cards

I've been making handmade cards since I was a kid. I'm inherently frugal and hate to spend an exorbitant amount for a purchased card. I prefer making a one-of-a-kind card mostly because it's my way of expressing my affection for the recipient. And there's a little quiet missionary zeal going on here, too: By passing on a hand-embroidered card, I can spread the word that embroidery is a fascinating, creative craft!

It may seem odd to apply the supple quality of thread to rigid paper, but stiff paper decorated with textural stitches done in glossy or fluffy threads adds a third dimension to what we're used to seeing as a flat, printed item. Keep the cards simple, and make a bunch of them at a time, so you have them ready to send when the occasion occurs. The same designs and techniques shown here for cards are perfect for scrapbook pages, as well.

starflower orange card

The stitches that work best on paper are Running Stitch, Backstitch, French Knots, and Straight Stitch. Because paper is stiff you'll have to re-invent "scoop" stitches, such as Lazy Daisy and Chain Stitches, by breaking them into two steps.

FINISHED SIZE: 5½ x 8½" card

GROUND

One 8½" x 11" piece of card stock *each* in orange and lime green

6" x 9" envelope in two coordinating colors

THREAD

Assorted colors of 6-strand cotton embroidery floss in three colors.

I used Anchor 102 (purple), 9046 (red), and 256 (lime green).

NOTIONS

Size 18 chenille needle

Tape

Glue

STITCHES

French Knot (page 29)

Straight Stitch (page 22)

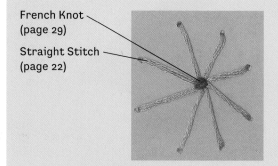

PREPARING THE PAPER

1. Measure and cut the orange card stock to 4" × 6½".
2. Mark the positions of the starflower centers by using pencil to lightly mark six points, randomly spaced.
3. Use the needle to poke holes through the marked points and five to eight holes randomly spaced in a circle around each center. The diameter of my starflowers varied from ¾" to 1½". These are your stitching holes.

STITCHING THE DESIGN

4. Using six strands of lime green, purple, and red, work star-shaped flowers in Straight Stitch, moving from each center point to the randomly spaced holes around it. Leave 1" of thread at the back; do not knot the thread. After stitching, pull the thread to the back of the card, cut the thread, and tape both thread ends to the back of the card stock.
5. In random colors, work French Knots in the center of each flower.

FINISHING THE CARD

6. Tape all ends in place. Fold the lime green cardstock in half widthwise (it will measure 5½" × 8½"). Center the orange embroidered card over the front of the folded lime green card, and glue it in place.
7. Write a note and send it to a friend.

flower-and-dot yellow card

If you find stitching on paper too restrictive, do your stitches on a small piece of fabric and then glue the fabric to the card. Or, if you're particularly proud of a beautiful embroidery you did on a pillow or other object, photocopy it and apply the copy to a card to make completely original stationery.

FINISHED SIZE: 5½ x 8½" card

GROUND

One 8½" x 11" piece of cardstock *each* in yellow and hot pink

6" x 9" envelope in lime green

THREAD

Assorted colors of 6-strand cotton embroidery floss.

I used Anchor 925 (orange), 88 (fuchsia), and 256 (lime green).

NOTIONS

Size 18 chenille needle

Tape

Glue

STITCHES

French Knot
(page 29)

Lazy Daisy
(page 27)

PREPARING THE PAPER

1. Measure and cut the yellow cardstock to 4" × 6½".
2. Use a see-through ruler and pencil to measure and very lightly mark a vertical line down center of card. Measure and mark center point of this line. Mark points 1½" away from center point in both directions. The flower centers will go here. (See diagram on page 198).
3. Use a needle to poke five holes from front to back, randomly spaced around each center point. These are your stitching points at the tip of each petal.

STITCHING THE DESIGN

4. Using six strands of orange embroidery cotton, work a lazy daisy with five petals at the center flower mark. Work the Lazy Daisy Stitch in four parts, as follows:
   a. Come up to right side at center and draw thread through.
   b. Go back down, leaving a long loop on front.
   c. Come up at one of the holes for tip of petal, poking the threaded needle through the loop and pulling gently.
   d. Go to back through the same hole to finish the petal. Arrange petal so it is neat. Repeat these steps for all five petals, finishing on inside. Tape end and trim.
5. With green, work a Lazy Daisy in each of the two remaining flower holes.
6. With orange, work a French Knot in the center of each flower. (It's okay to come up and go down in the same hole when you're working a French Knot on paper.)
7. Poke 12 holes, randomly spaced, on the paper. With orange, work French Knots in each hole.

FINISHING THE CARD

8. Erase any pencils marks. Tape all ends in place. Fold the hot pink cardstock in half widthwise (it will measure 5½" × 8½"). Center the yellow embroidered card over the front of the folded hot pink card, and glue it in place.

Scissors Case and Charm

I enclose my sharp-pointed embroidery scissors in this pretty little hand-stitched case to avoid being stabbed by them when I'm fishing around in my project bag. The case, along with a pair of elegant embroidery scissors, is a wonderful gift for an accomplished stitcher or someone who's just learning. To easily identify my scissors when I'm with a group, I embroider a little charm with my initial or a flower and hang it from one of the scissors handles. Before I discovered this trick, I returned home many an evening from a stitch-and-bitch session to find someone else's scissors in my bag.

To make the braid, cut an 18" piece of 3-ply Persian wool, and thread it through a needle. Draw it through the fabric as directed in the instructions (step 8) at the right; unthread the needle. Pull the two ends parallel and hold them together. Hold the case or charm between your knees (or have someone else hold it for you). Holding the threads taut, separate the plies, grouping two plies together, so that you have three pairs of plies. Braid the three pieces together until the braid measures 6". Make an overhand knot at the end of the braid and trim the tail.

FINISHED SIZE: 5 ¾" x 3" (closed)

FABRIC

Small scraps of recycled wool blanket, sweater, or coating fabric in two fun colors, washed and felted (see page 46)

THREAD

One 8-yard, 3-ply skein of Persian wool in *each* of two, pretty, contrasting colors.

I used Paternayan, Purple/331 and Hot Pink/961.

NOTIONS

Size 20 chenille needle

STITCHES

A Blanket Stitch (page 26)

B French Knot (page 29)

C Lazy Daisy (page 27)

D Stem Stitch (page 25)

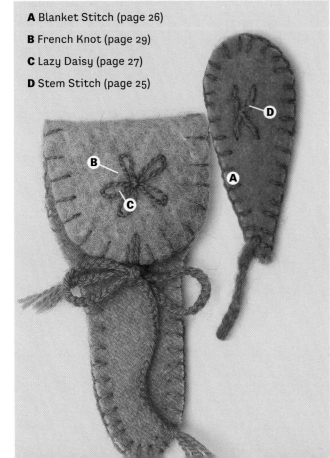

PREPARING THE FABRIC

1. Use a photocopier to enlarge the Scissors Case patterns on page 197 by 200%. Cut patterns out.
2. Using a different color fabric for each piece, place patterns for front and back of case on fabric, and trace around them with a water-soluble or child's washable marker; cut pieces out. Cut two pieces from charm pattern; draw an initial centered on one of these pieces.

STITCHING THE DESIGN

Use one strand of wool for all stitches.

3. Work Blanket Stitch across the straight edge of the smaller piece for the case.
4. Pin the two pieces of the case together, matching the bottom edges. Beginning at the right straight edge, work Blanket Stitch to stitch the two pieces together. Continue Blanket Stitch all the way around the flap.
5. Work a Lazy Daisy in the center of the outside of the flap. Work a French Knot in the center of the daisy.
6. Work the outline of the initial on the charm in Stem Stitch.
7. Pin the two charm pieces together, wrong sides facing. Work Blanket Stitch all the way around, enclosing any knots and ends between the two layers of fabric.

FINISHING THE SCISSORS CASE

8. **Flap braid.** Make a braid (see facing page), and draw it through the fabric at the center of the flap ½" in from edge.
9. **Lower case braid.** Make another braid, drawing the thread through the fabric at the center 1½" down from the straight edge of the smaller case piece. Bring both ends toward the front of the work (both ends are on top of the fabric).
10. **Charm.** Make another braid, attaching the yarn to the charm about ⅜" from the point. Tie the charm to one of the scissor handles.
11. Neaten the thread ends by trimming to ¼", and remove all marking lines. Block (see page 21).

Embellished Espadrilles

When I first ventured to Europe in my early twenties, I saw chic, artfully dressed women wearing espadrilles, which could be found at every outdoor market. I still love wearing espadrilles in the summer. I was delighted to find these handmade Spanish shoes on the Internet in lots of fun colors.

I've always coveted high-end embroidered shoes, but they are simply out of my budget. So, I've worked simple embroidery on my inexpensive Spanish espadrilles, adding flair to something everyone can afford. I became so entranced that I made a child-sized pair for my daughter, Julia, too.

FINISHED SIZE To fit

FABRIC

Two pairs "Carmen" classic Spanish espadrilles, one adult size and one child size (see Resources for ordering information)

THREAD

One 8.7-yard, 6-strand skein *each* of cotton embroidery floss in two colors.

I used Anchor 89 (fuchsia) and 238 (green).

NOTIONS

Size 18 chenille needle for Child shoe; Size 20 chenille needle for Adult shoe

STITCHES

A French Knot (page 29)

B Running Stitch (page 23)

C Lazy Daisy (page 27)

STITCHING THE DESIGN

Because of the shape of the espadrilles, you will need to "eyeball" all the stitching (page 85). Use all six strands of embroidery floss throughout.

1. *For the adult's shoe,* using fuchsia, work two rows of Running Stitch along the two straight edges of the shoe, placing the first close to the edge and the second ½" in from the edge. *For the child's shoe,* work one row of Running Stitch along the two straight edges of the shoe close to the edge. Make the stitches about ¼" long. Anchor the beginning and ending threads securely so they won't pop through to the outside of the shoe.

2. *For the adult's shoe,* using green, work French Knots between the rows of Running Stitch, spacing the knots ⅜" apart.

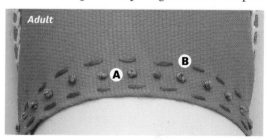

For the child's shoe, using fuchsia, work a Lazy Daisy flower at the center top of the espadrille. Using green, work three French Knots in the center of the Lazy Daisy flower.

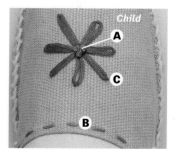

FINISHING THE SHOES

3. Neaten the thread ends by trimming to ¼", and remove all marking lines. Use a steam iron to press the shoes and even out the stitching; spritz with extra water, as needed.

Be-ribboned pillows

By now, you've discovered that you can do embroidery on many non-traditional types of fabrics, with many kinds of threads. I used common grosgrain ribbon and seam binding tape as "threads" for these whimsical, quick-to-make pillows. The green pillow features grosgrain ribbon tied in square knots to form a simple, tailored, block design. I worked the seam binding on the gold pillow in a simple Running Stitch to create a shimmering diagonal plaid.

Embroidering with ribbons is a very popular form of stitchery. If you enjoy making these pillows, look for the wide assortment of books written solely about ribbon embroidery. Entire companies have formed to sell ribbon, needles, and other tools for ribbon embroidery. A rich world of embroidery is ripe for exploration!

tied pillow

FINISHED SIZE: 14" x 14"

FABRIC

½ yard green, wool blanket or coating fabric, for pillow front

½ yard cotton fabric, for pillow back

THREAD

2 yards of ⅜"-wide grosgrain ribbon

NOTIONS

Size 14 yarn darning needle

14" square pillow insert (preferably down)

PREPARING THE PILLOW FRONT AND BACK

1. Measure and cut a 17" square (see page 44).
2. Measure and cut pillow back fabric for either a non-removable cover or a flapped back opening for a 14" square pillow (see page 48). Set pillow back aside.
3. Referring to diagram on page 198, use a pin or a water-soluble or child's washable marker to mark center and eight other points, each 4" apart. (For tips on finding center, see page 18.)

STITCHING THE DESIGN

4. Cut nine pieces of ribbon, 6" long. Thread a needle with a piece of ribbon and draw it through fabric at one of the marks, going from front to back and back to front; take up about ¼" with your stitch. Tie a square knot (see box, below).
5. Repeat for the eight other ties.
6. Trim ends of each ribbon on a diagonal, to about 2" long.

FINISHING THE PILLOW

7. Remove marking lines. Block and press completed pillow front as shown on page 21.
8. Keeping design centered, trim pillow front to 15" square.
9. With right sides facing, stitch the front and back together, taking a ½" seam allowance and following the instructions on pages 48–49 for the type of backing you chose.
10. Stuff with pillow insert.

it's okay to be square

Take an end of ribbon in each hand. Loop right end over left and bring it under. Loop left end over right and bring it under. ("Right over left and left over right, makes a knot neat, tidy, and tight.")

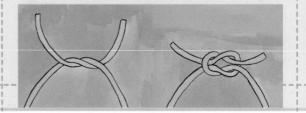

diamonds and gold

It's said that "diamonds are a girl's best friend," and this sparkling design proves that diamonds and gold are even better.

FINISHED SIZE: 12" x 12"

FABRICS

½ yard gold wool blanket or coating fabric, for pillow front

½ yard of cotton fabric, for pillow back

THREAD

Two 5-yard packages of hot pink, non-fusible seam binding

NOTIONS

Size 14 yarn darning needle

12" pillow insert (preferably down)

PREPARING THE PILLOW FRONT AND BACK

1. Measure and cut a 15" square for the pillow front. (For tips on cutting a square, see page 44.)
2. Measure and cut the pillow back fabric for either a non-removable cover or a flapped back opening for a 12"-square pillow. (See page 48.) Set pillow back aside.
3. Referring to the diagram on page 198, use a see-through ruler and a water-soluble or child's washable marker to draw five diagonal lines in each direction, spaced 3" apart, centered on the pillow, and forming a diagonal plaid.
4. Iron the seam binding flat to remove the folds.

STITCHING THE DESIGN

5. Using the yarn darning needle and a length of seam binding, work large Running Stitches along one of the lines, making the stitches float on top of the fabric for about 1¼" and taking a small (¼") stitch on the backside of the fabric.
6. Repeat on the other nine lines.

FINISHING THE PILLOW

7. Neaten the thread ends by trimming to ¼", and remove all marking lines. Block and press the completed piece (see page 21). Press with the embroidered side facing down. Take care not to press so hard that the ribbon gets too flattened.
8. Keeping the design centered, trim the pillow front piece to 13" square.
9. With right sides facing, stitch the front and back together, taking a ½" seam allowance and following the instructions of pages 48–49 for the type of backing you chose.
10. Stuff with pillow insert.

Sources for Supplies

PATERNAYAN PERSIAN WOOL

JCA
35 Scales Lane
West Townsend, MA 01469
508.597.8794

COTTON FLOSS AND PEARL COTTON

Anchor Threads
Coats & Clark
P.O. Box 12229
Greenville, SC 29612
800.648.1479

www.coatsandclark.com

DMC
10 Port Kearny
South Kearny, NJ 07032
973.589.0606

www.dmc-usa.com

Julia Handknitting Yarn
Westminster Fibers
4 Townsend West
Nashua NH 03063
800.445.9276

DYES

Rupert, Gibbon & Spider, Inc.
P.O. Box 425
Healdsburg, CA 95448
Toll Free: 800.442.0455

www.jacquardproducts.com

WOOL FELT

Magic Cabin
P.O. Box 1049
Madison, VA 22727
888.623.6556

www.magiccabin.com

BLANKET REMNANTS FOR DYEING

Faribault Woolen Mill Store
1819 2nd Ave., NW
Faribault, MN 55021
Phone: 800.448.9665

www.faribowool.com

FABRICS

Osgood Textile Company
333 Park St.
West Springfield, MA 01089
888.674.6638

www.osgoodtextile.com

Delectable Mountain Cloth
125 Main St.
Brattleboro, Vermont 05301
802.257.4456

www.delectablemountain.com

B & J Fabrics
263 West 40th St.
New York, NY 10018
212.354.8150

Fishman's Fabrics
1101 S Desplaines St.
Chicago, 60607
312.922.7250

www.fishmansfabrics.com

Rosen & Chadick
246 West 40th St.
NY, NY 10018
212.869.0142

ESPADRILLES

www.espadrillesetc.com
Fax: 34 965 690 265
In Spain, by phone: 34.965.690.158

Style 'Carmen' is available in oodles of colors!

RIBBONS

VV Rouleaux
54 Sloane Square
London, England
SW1W 8AX
44.020.7730.3125

www.vvrouleaux.com

EMBROIDERY SCISSORS

Garrett and Wade
161 Avenue of the Americas
New York, NY 10013
800.221.2942

www.garrettwade.com

Websites

www.embroideryarts.com
www.sublimestitching.com

Museums

These have especially great textile collections.

Victoria and Albert Museum, London

Museum of Fine Arts, Boston

Metropolitan Museum of Art, New York

RISD Art Museum, Providence, RI

The Textile Museum, Washington, DC

Paisley Shawl Museum, Paisley, Scotland

Inspirational Reading

Bossert, Helmuth Th., *Folk Art of Asia, Africa, Australia, and the Americas* (Rizzoli, 1990)

Bossert, Helmuth Theodor, *Treasury of Historic Folk Ornament* (Dover Publications, 1996; reprint of a 1924 German edition)

Gillow, John, and Bryan Sentence, *World Textiles* (Bulfinch Press, 1999)

Jones, Owen, *The Grammar of Ornament* (Dover Publications, 1987; reprint of an 1856 book on decoration through the centuries)

Kennett, Frances, with Caroline MacDonald-Haig, *Ethnic Dress* (Conran Octopus, 1994)

Meller, Susan, and Joost Elffers, *Textile Designs* (Harry N. Abrams, 1991)

Paine, Sheila, *Embroidered Textiles* (Thames and Hudson, 1990)

Tilke, Max, *Costume Patterns and Designs* (Rizzoli, 1990)

Tilke, Max, *National Costumes from East Europe, Africa, and Asia* (Hastings House, 1978)

Metric Conversions

TO GET	WHEN YOU KNOW	MULTIPLY BY
centimeters	inches	2.54
meters	feet	0.305
meters	yards	0.9144

FREQUENTLY USED MEASUREMENTS

INCHES	CENTIMETERS	INCHES	CENTIMETERS	INCHES	CENTIMETERS	INCHES	CENTIMETERS
0.5	1.27	6.5	16.51	15	38.10	27	68.58
1	2.54	7	17.78	16	40.64	28	71.12
1.5	3.81	7.5	19.05	17	43.18	29	73.66
2	5.08	8	20.32	18	45.72	30	76.20
2.5	6.35	8.5	21.59	19	48.26	31	78.74
3	7.62	9	22.86	20	50.80	32	81.28
3.5	8.89	9.5	24.13	21	53.34	33	83.82
4	10.16	10	25.40	22	55.88	34	86.36
4.5	11.43	11	27.94	23	58.42	35	88.90
5	12.70	12	30.48	24	60.96	36	91.44
5.5	13.97	13	33.02	25	63.50		
6	15.24	14	35.56	26	66.04		

ACKNOWLEDGMENTS

I couldn't have created this book without the support I have had all of my life from my mom and dad, Arch and Nancy Nicholas, and my four sisters, Lynn Nicholas, Laurie Nicholas Rabe, Nancy Belletete, and Jennifer Nicholas. Without their encouragement, faith in my skills (and often wacky ideas), and sometimes (lots of times) even physical help, I wouldn't have learned to create the beautiful textiles that I have built a life around. It helps to have loving hands around you.

Thanks to Kevin Kennefick for his beautiful pictures, Sheri Riddell for all her smiling upbeat assistance during the photo shoot, and Wendy Scofield for her styling ways and for making my photo dreams come true. Yes, even that little chick (who is now busily laying eggs for that egg cozy). Thanks, too, to my mom, Nancy, who happily kept us all fed and nurtured during the shoot and to Gwen Steege, my editor, for her calming demeanor during mayhem.

Thanks to the following, who helped me complete some of the projects: my sisters and their daughters, Nancy and Celia Belletete and Laurie and Olivia Rabe; my mom, Nancy K. Nicholas; and my friends Candi Jensen, Clara Lopez, Kay Dougherty, Gwen Steege, and Cathy Payson. Thanks to Lori Gayle for keeping my website spiffy and colorful. A special thanks to my great friends who are always there for me and who share the passion of textiles: Sally Lee, Linda Pratt, and Cathy Payson.

Thanks to the following embroiderers for their help in stitching a lot of bookmarks for regional trade shows: Mamie Anthoine Ney, Jane Whitney, Constance Loring, Laurie Sims, Barbara Yocom, Deborah Sinclair, Pat Sweet, Gail Metzger, Debby Wolak, Gloria Riordan, Carol Auger, Tara Beshai, Mary Brinton, Debby Baker, KathyAnn Heckman, Jasia Chmielewski, and Kelli Kozak.

Thanks to all the companies who supplied me with materials for stitching, especially Alan Getz from JCA, who has also produced The Kristin Nicholas Collection of Stitchery Kits.

The team at Storey had faith in my vision that stitchery could be fun and creative. Pam Art, Deborah Balmuth, Kent Lew, and Cindy McFarland, along with many others, have produced this book before you. Gwen Steege, my editor, cheered me on and then organized the confusion all with a smile. To all of them I am very grateful.

Lastly, thanks and love to my husband, Mark Duprey, who knows how important the confusion and chaos is to my creativity, and to my daughter, Julia, who keeps me amazed as she travels through life.

project patterns and diagrams

The following pages contain the diagrams and patterns referred to in the project instructions. The *diagrams* show measurements for stitching guidelines, seams, fold lines, and placement of patterns. (For information on how to measure and center designs, see pages 13–14.) The *patterns* provide stitching guidelines and/or project shapes. All of the patterns must be enlarged. Use a photocopier (available at office supply stores) for this purpose, entering the percentage for enlargement indicated on each pattern. (For information about photocopying and transferring patterns to fabric, see pages 13–15.) *Note:* Storey Publishing grants permission to reproduce the patterns on pages 184–98 for personal use only.

overlapping dots

(page 61)   ENLARGE 333%

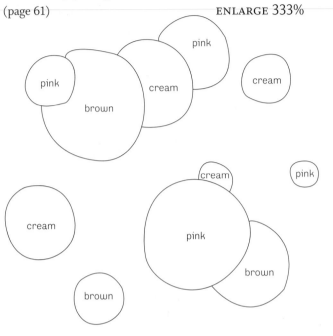

under-the-sea coral

(page 64)   ENLARGE 333%

Tuscan trees

(page 63)   ENLARGE 200%

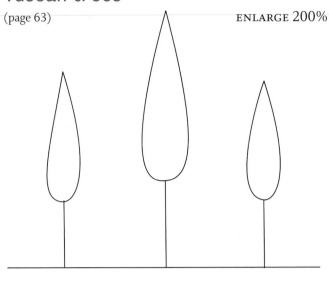

loopy vine

(page 65)   ENLARGE 500%

creativity/chaos

(page 69) ENLARGE 286%

checks with crewel flowers

(page 92) ENLARGE 333%

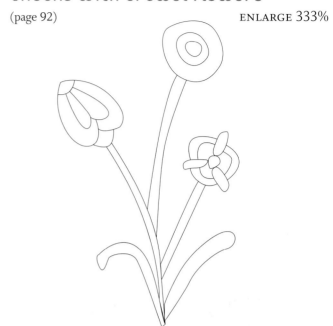

plaid with flowers

(page 94) ENLARGE 500%

mini-stripes and flowers

(page 97) ENLARGE 333%

dragonfly
(page 102)

ENLARGE 200%

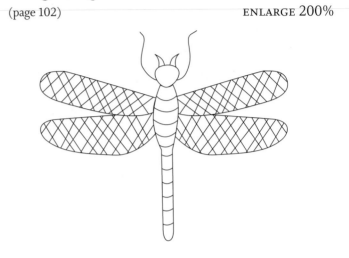

undulating vines on stripes
(page 99)   23" × 23"

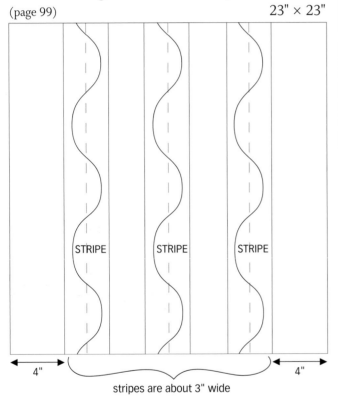

4"

STRIPE   STRIPE   STRIPE

4"

stripes are about 3" wide

moth
(page 104)

ENLARGE 167%

ENLARGE 286%

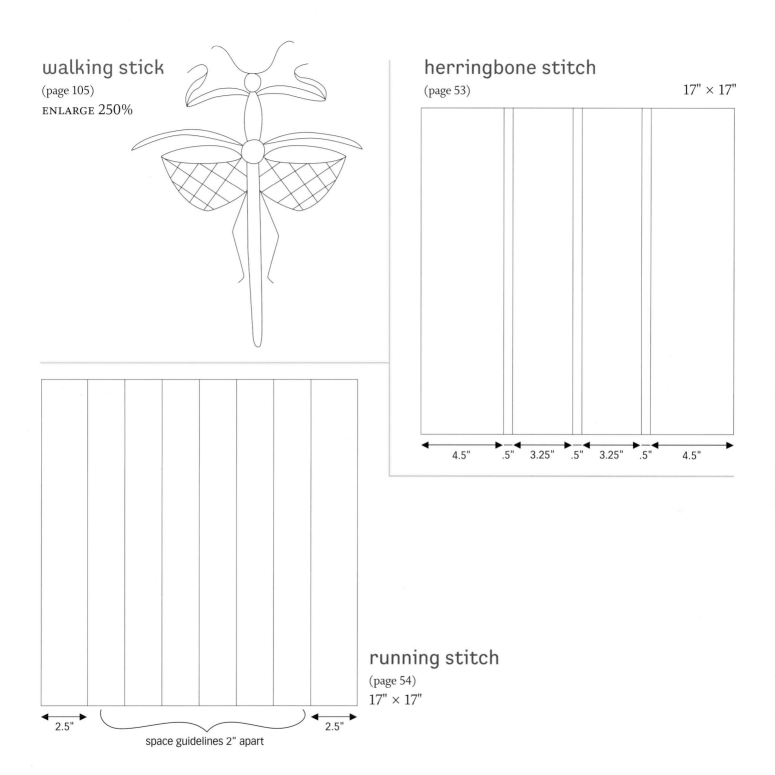

walking stick

(page 105)

ENLARGE 250%

herringbone stitch

(page 53)

17" × 17"

4.5"   .5"   3.25"   .5"   3.25"   .5"   4.5"

running stitch

(page 54)

17" × 17"

2.5"   2.5"

space guidelines 2" apart

chain stitch

(page 55)   17" × 17"

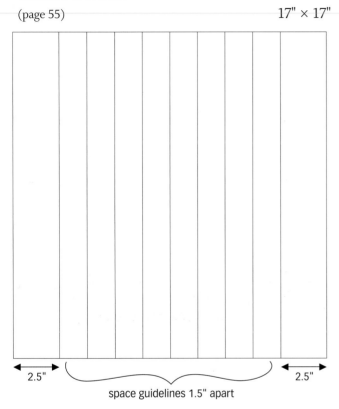

2.5"   space guidelines 1.5" apart   2.5"

sampler stripes

(page 71)   19" × 19"

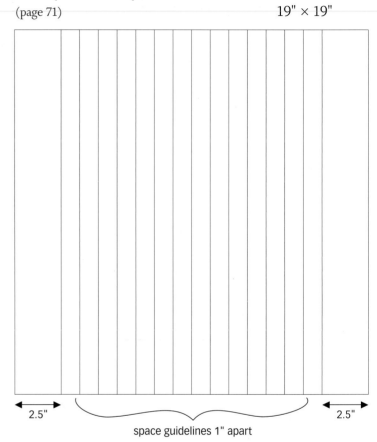

2.5"   space guidelines 1" apart   2.5"

green-and-white gingham and blue-and-white gingham (page 75–76)

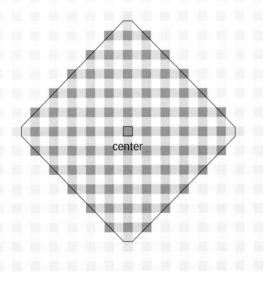

center

fern & backstitch on pink

(page 72)
17" × 17"

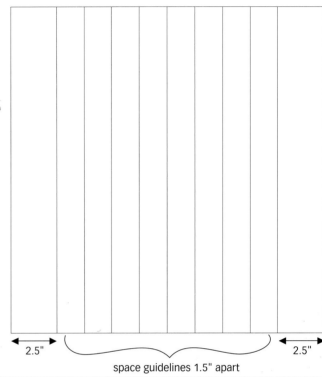

2.5" space guidelines 1.5" apart 2.5"

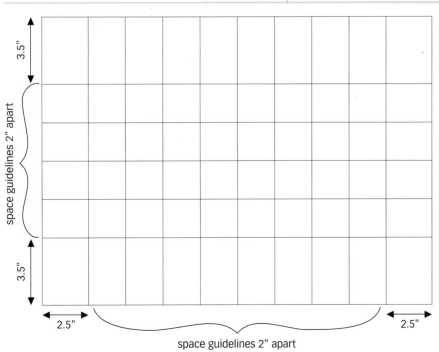

3.5"

space guidelines 2" apart

3.5"

2.5" space guidelines 2" apart 2.5"

French knot plaid

(page 73)
15" × 21"

blue-and-white windowpane plaid

(page 79)   17" × 17"

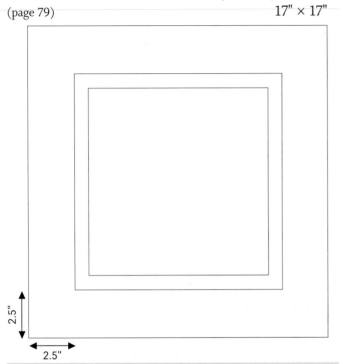

2.5"

2.5"

not-so-lazy daisies

(page 98)   21" ×
21"

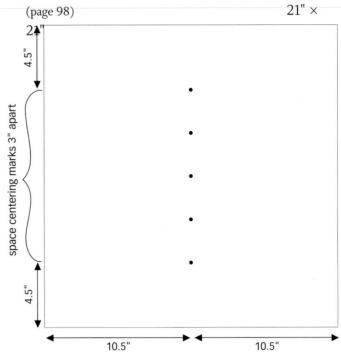

4.5"

space centering marks 3" apart

4.5"

10.5"   10.5"

green-and-white
windowpane plaid

(page 80)

19" × 19"

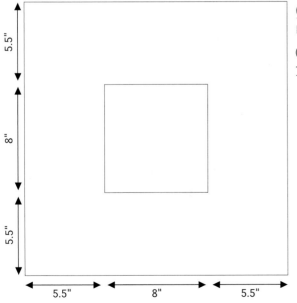

5.5"

8"

5.5"

5.5"   8"   5.5"

tea cozy

(page 110)

ENLARGE
500%

cut 4 for cozy
cut 2 for lining
cut 2 for interfacing

a good-egg cozy

(page 112)

ENLARGE 200%

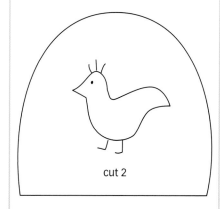

cut 2

sunflower napkins

(page 121)

ENLARGE
167%

sunflower tablecloth

(page 120)

ENLARGE 250%

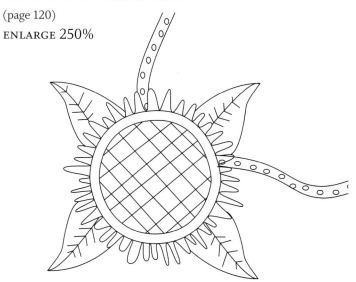

DIAGRAM FOR PLACEMENT

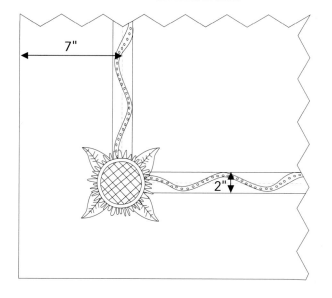

7"

2"

bistro

(page 124)

ENLARGE 250%

bistro

café julia

(page 125)

ENLARGE 250%

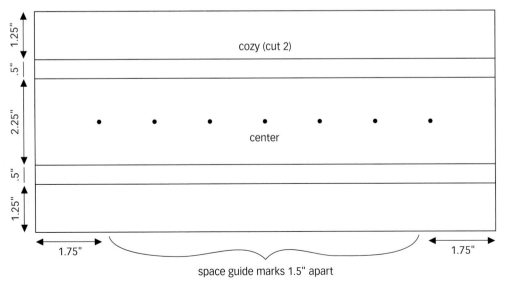

cozy (cut 2)

center

1.25"

.5"

2.25"

.5"

1.25"

1.75"

1.75"

space guide marks 1.5" apart

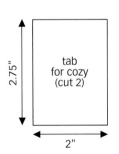

tab
for cozy
(cut 2)

2.75"

2"

coffee cozy

(page 111)

ENLARGE 245%

12.5" × 5.75"

swirly border

(page 131)

43" × 37"

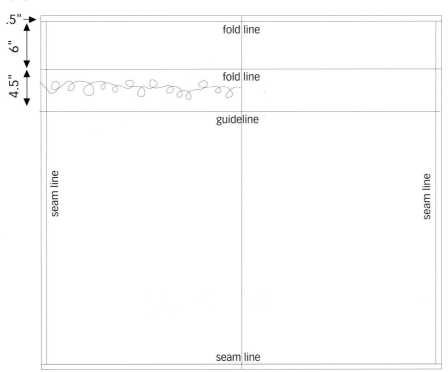

.5"

6"

4.5"

fold line

fold line

guideline

seam line

seam line

seam line

ENLARGE 250%

it's a mod, mod flowered world

(page 132)

43" × 37"

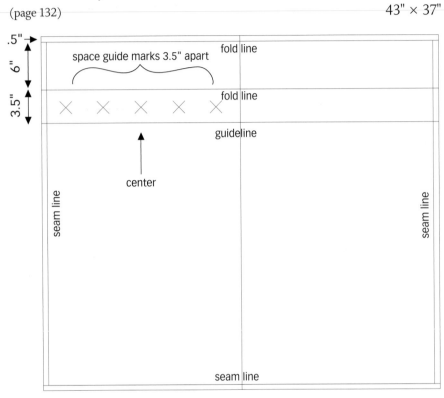

ENLARGE 167%

four-petaled flower

(page 139)

ENLARGE 250%

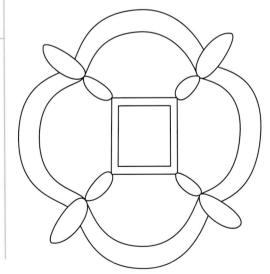

blanketed with love

(page 145)

ENLARGE 250%

please stitch the daisies

(page 133)

43" × 37"

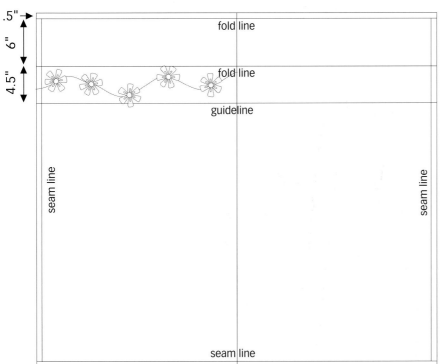

ENLARGE 250%

golden sea of wildflowers

(page 136)   ENLARGE 400%

his-and-hers cozies

(page 158)

ENLARGE 200%

heart-to-heart pillow

(page 155)

ENLARGE 500%

striped vase with flowers

(page 140)

ENLARGE 333%

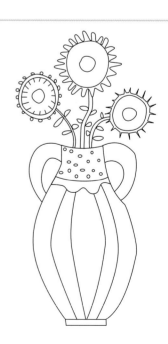

julia's teddy bears

(page 146)

ENLARGE EACH PIECE 250%

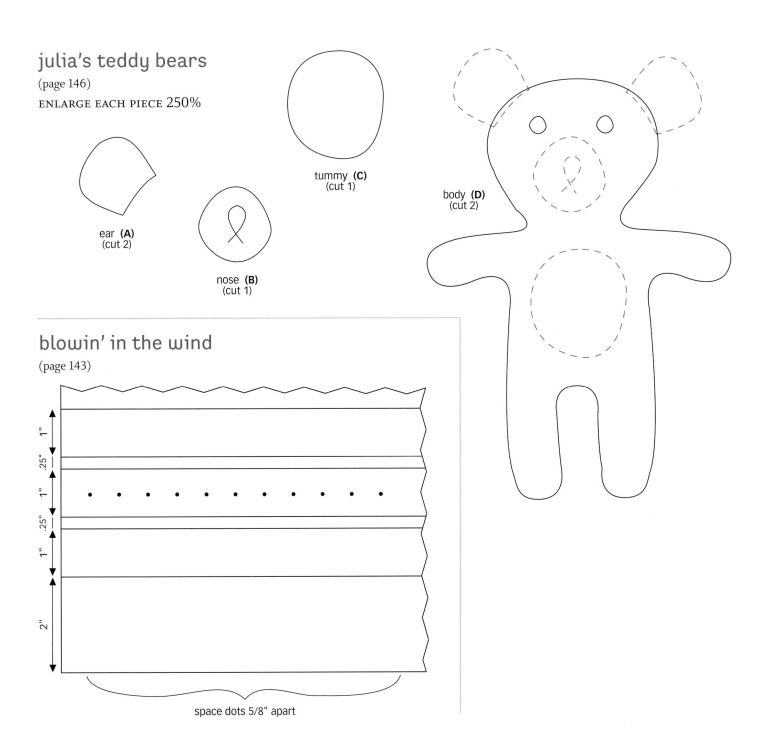

ear **(A)**
(cut 2)

nose **(B)**
(cut 1)

tummy **(C)**
(cut 1)

body **(D)**
(cut 2)

blowin' in the wind

(page 143)

1"

.25"

1"

.25"

1"

2"

space dots 5/8" apart

wedding blanket

(page 154)

ENLARGE 200%

Letters= 3"
Date= 1.5"

edge of blanket

8.5"

9.5"

Names
Date

8.5"

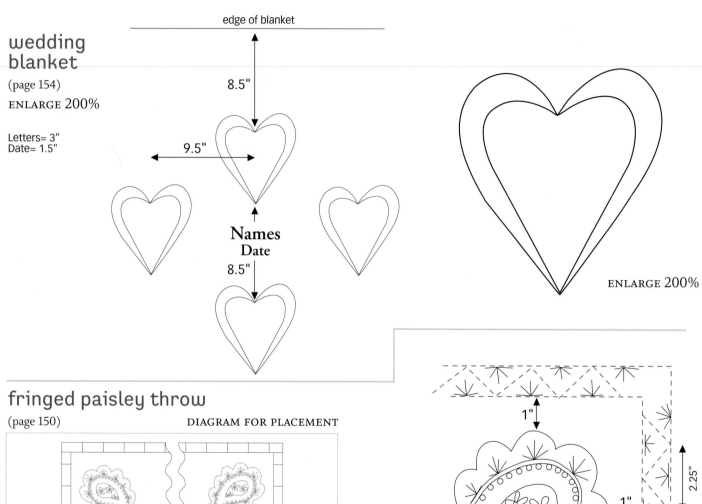

ENLARGE 200%

fringed paisley throw

(page 150)

DIAGRAM FOR PLACEMENT

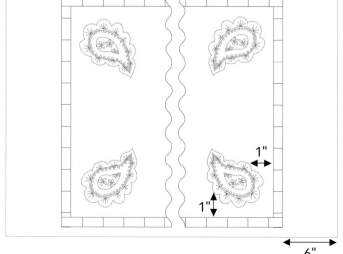

1"

1"

6"

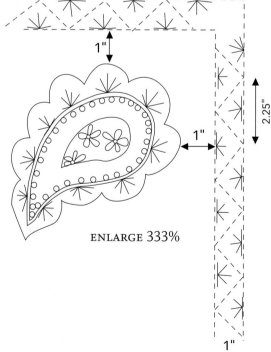

1"

2.25"

1"

ENLARGE 333%

1"

circular periwinkle box

(page 163)   ENLARGE 250%

8" DIAMETER

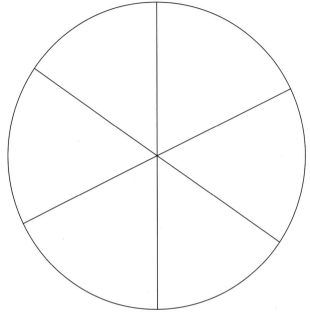

six-sided green box

(page 164)   ENLARGE 250%

7.75" DIAMETER, FLAT SIDE TO FLAT SIDE, 9" ON DIAGONAL

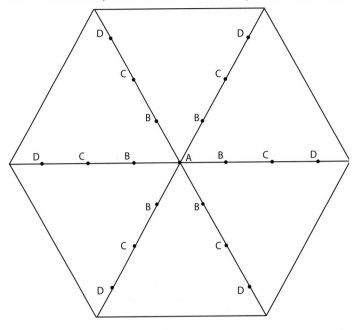

scissors case & charm

(page 171)   ENLARGE ALL 3 PIECES 200%

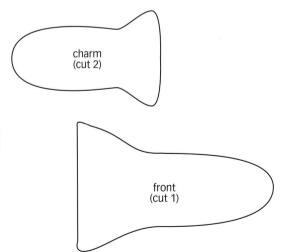

back
(cut 1)

charm
(cut 2)

front
(cut 1)

six-sided pink box (page 165) ENLARGE 286%

8.5" DIAMETER FLAT SIDE TO FLAT SIDE, 9.75" DIAGONAL

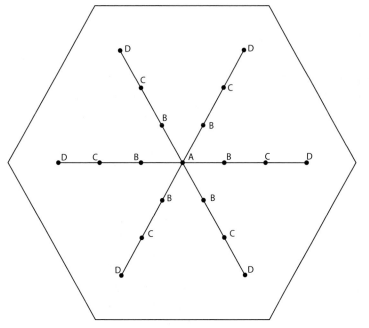

diamonds and gold

(page 177) ENLARGE 500% 15" × 15"

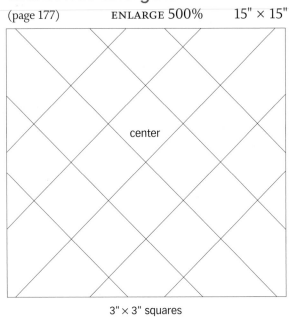

center

3" × 3" squares

tied pillow

(page 176)
17" × 17"

4.5" 4" 4" 4.5"

center

flower-and-dot yellow card

(page 169)
4" × 6.5"

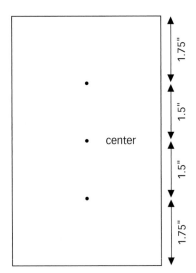

center

1.75" 1.5" 1.5" 1.75"

Index

Page numbers in *italics* indicate photographs or illustrations. Page numbers in **bold** indicate tables.

Other Storey Titles You Will Enjoy

Knit One, Felt Too by Kathleen Taylor
Twenty-five easy-to-master felted knitting patterns will have knitters turning out colorful, cozy mittens, socks, gifts, and accessories. The projects all use the same simple yet magical steps — knit the project large and loose, wash it in hot water, and see it transformed into a soft, thick wool felt.
176 pages. Paperback ISBN 1-58017-497-3.

Hooked on Crochet by Candi Jensen
Fully illustrated, step-by-step instructions and full-color photographs take crocheters through 20 fun projects, including hip hats, bold bags, swinging scarves, and fabulous home accessories.
144 pages. Paperback ISBN 1-58017-547-3.

At Knit's End by Stephanie Pearl-McPhee
The tangled life of the obsessive knitter is the subject of inspired nuttiness in 300 tongue-in-cheek meditations on the excuses, rationales, trials, and tribulations common to all women who knit far too much!
320 pages. Paperback ISBN 1-58017-589-9.

Knit & Crochet Ponchos, Wraps, Capes & Shrugs! edited by Edie Eckman
This collection covers the gamut of popular wrap options with 16 patterns ranging from a comfy Aran Panel knitted poncho to an elegant Cinderella Cape, all featuring step-by-step instructions.
144 pages. Hardcover ISBN 1-58017-621-6

Knit Scarves! by Candi Jensen
Nothing is simpler than knitting a colorful, cozy scarf, and scarves just don't get any prettier or more fun than they are here, with 16 patterns and advice on everything from choosing the proper needles to experimenting with dozens of alternative and novelty yarn choices.
96 pages. Hardcover ISBN 1-58017-577-5.

Crochet Scarves! by Candi Jensen
Easy enough for beginners but fun enough for experienced crocheters, these 16 projects make wonderful use of a popular array of yarns — wool, mohair, novelty acrylic yarns, soft cottons — to create scarves for every taste.
96 pages. Hardcover ISBN 1-58017-620-8.

These and other books from Storey Publishing are available wherever quality books are sold or by calling 1-800-441-5700. Visit us at www.storey.com

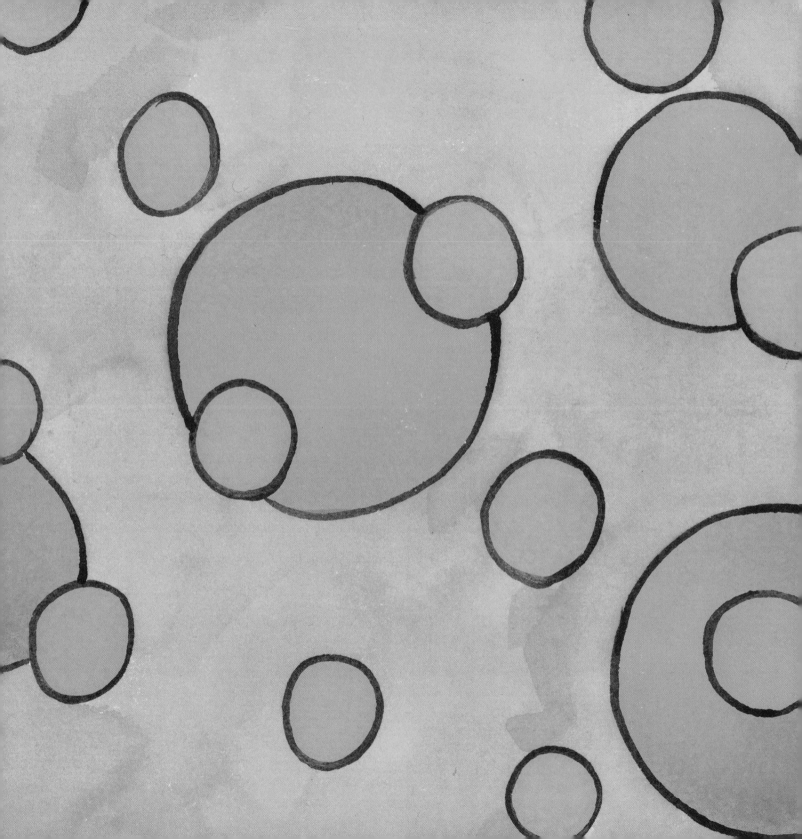

Artist and needlework designer Kristin Nicholas' designs and home have been featured in *Country Home* and *House and Garden* magazines, as well as on the syndicated television program *Martha Stewart Living.* Her stitchery designs, "The Kristin Nicholas Collection," are distributed by JCA and available as kits at stitchery stores nationwide. She has written and illustrated several previous books. Kristin resides in western Massachusetts in an antique farmhouse in an abandoned apple orchard with her husband and daughter and an ever-growing menagerie of dogs, cats, chickens, pigs, and 150 sheep. Her work can be seen on her website, www.kristinnicholas.com.